Mentoring for Success

Elizabeth Weinstein, Ph.D.

Provant Media Publishing
4601 121ST Street
Urbandale IA, 50323-2311
1-888-776-8268
www.provantmedia.com

Mentoring for Success

Elizabeth Weinstein, Ph.D.
Copyright © 1998 by Provant Media

This publication is designed to provide accurate and authoritative information in regard to the subject matter covered. It is sold with the understanding that neither the author nor the publisher is engaged in rendering legal, accounting, or other professional service. If legal advice or other expert assistance is required, the services of a competent professional should be sought.

Credits:

Provant Media Publishing:	Art Bauer
	Todd McDonald
Editor in Chief:	Karen Massetti Miller
Designer:	Michelle Glass
Cover Design and Illustration:	Kevin Zdenek

Published by Provant Media
4601 121ST Street
Urbandale IA, 50323-2311

Library of Congress Catalog Card Number 98-72663
Weinstein, Elizabeth, Ph.D.
Mentoring for Success

ISBN 1-884926-94-0

Printed in the United States of America
01 00 99 98   9 8 7 6 5 4 3 2 1

Introduction

Today's workplace is exciting, vibrant, and constantly changing. Information that is relevant today is outmoded tomorrow. Businesses and organizations are no longer dealing with customers from their own communities—or even their countries—but are interacting with others from around the world. The global economy is possible because of the extraordinary growth in worldwide communication and the ease of long-distance travel. There has also been a shift in the type of work businesses do. Information and service industries are expanding dramatically.

In order for businesses to survive and remain competitive, they must respond to this changing environment. As Tom Peters observes in *Thriving on Chaos,* "Excellent firms don't believe in excellence—only in constant improvement and constant change." As part of their response to change, successful organizations seek ways to support and foster employee growth and development. Managers are developing skills to facilitate this process. They are acting as mentors to their employees. Coworkers and other employees with company experience and skills are also offering their services as mentors to less-experienced employees.

In addition, nonprofit groups, government agencies, and educational organizations are relying increasingly on mentoring as a means to assist young people by providing role models for both social and educational purposes. The movement from welfare to work has also created some innovative mentoring programs to help individuals break away from the welfare system.

This book considers both formal mentoring, which is arranged, and informal mentoring, which simply evolves. It is designed for individuals who are charged with creating a mentoring program, for those who are contemplating entering a mentoring relationship and for those who are currently acting as mentors. We hope that clarifying the mentoring relationship will result in improved services to customers and increased employee productivity.

About the Author

Elizabeth Weinstein is the president of Elizabeth Weinstein and Associates, a training and consulting company based in Des Moines, Iowa.

Liz works with a variety of businesses, government agencies, and nonprofit organizations in a broad range of areas, including strategic planning, conflict management, and team building. Liz is also a project manager and most recently has been involved in interactive Web site development. In addition, Liz conducts research and develops manuals and other publications.

Liz has a bachelor's degree in elementary education from Buena Vista College, a master's degree from Creighton University, and a doctorate in community and human resources from the Unversity of Nebraska, Lincoln.

How to Use This Book

If you are charged with designing and implementing a mentoring program:

◆ Chapters 1 and 2 provide a background for developing your program.

◆ Chapter 3 takes you through a step-by-step process for creating a mentoring program.

◆ Chapter 4 offers descriptions of a sampling of existing mentoring programs.

◆ Chapter 5 offers creative strategies to address mentoring challenges.

If you are contemplating entering a mentoring relationship:

◆ Chapters 1 and 2 help you understand the benefits from mentoring and how the relationship should function.

◆ Chapter 5 provides an awareness of what challenges do exist in mentoring activities.

If you are currently in a mentoring relationship and are seeking to improve it:

◆ Chapters 1, 2, and 3 provide a review of the mentoring process and the benefits to be gained from effective mentor-mentee interactions.

◆ Chapter 5 identifies challenges that you might have encountered and gives suggestions about possible strategies to use.

What You Will Gain from This Book

If you are creating a mentoring program, you will be able to:

- Follow a step-by-step process for program development.

- Identify ways to "sell" your program.

- Discover how to recruit, train, and support mentors.

- Identify potential mentees and recruit them.

- Recognize problems in mentoring relationships.

- Learn strategies for giving mentee and mentor recognition.

- Measure the effectiveness of your mentoring program.

If you are about to become a mentor, you will be able to:

- Clarify the different roles you can play.

- Identify the DOs and DON'Ts of mentoring.

- Identify the skills you need to improve to be an effective mentor.

- Develop ideas on how to approach challenges that affect the mentoring relationship.

If you are seeking ways to improve your mentoring skills, you will be able to:

- Identify the level of your mentoring skills.

- Review the DOs and DON'Ts of mentoring actions.

- Find ideas on how to approach challenges that affect the mentoring relationship.

- View the mentoring interaction with a fresh eye.

Chapter One

What Is Mentoring?   8

Defining Mentoring   10
Tracing the History of Mentoring   12
Identifying the Qualities of a Mentor   13
Mastering the Four Roles of a Mentor   15
Chapter Summary   20
Self-Check: Chapter One Review   22

Chapter Two

Identifying Mentor Roles and Skills   24

Mentoring Self-Assessment   25
Developing the Skills of a Coach   28
Developing the Skills of a Consultant   32
Developing the Skills of a Teacher   36
Developing the Skills of a Relationship-Builder   42
Steps for Managing Conflict Constructively   45
Chapter Summary   47
Self Check: Chapter Two Review   48

Chapter Three

Creating a Formal Mentoring Program   50

Identifying the Characteristics of
    Formal Mentoring Programs   51
Designing and Proposing a Program   52
Recruiting and Matching Participants   62
Providing Orientation and Support   69
Evaluating Your Program   73
Chapter Summary   80
Self-Check: Chapter Three Review   82

Chapter Four

Models of Mentoring Programs 84

Model 1: FLIK Manager Trainee Program 85
Model 2: FLIK School-to-Work Program 87
Model 3: Hospital Youth Mentoring Program 89
Model 4: Cyanamid Agricultural Products
      Mentoring Program 93
Model 5: Iowa Volunteer Mentor Program 96
Model 6: Choices—Peer Education Program 100
Model 7: The Iowa Union-Based
      School-to-Work Mentoring Project 103
Model 8: Big Brothers/Big Sisters of
      Greater Des Moines, Iowa 107
Self-Check: Chapter Four Review 111

Chapter Five

Troubleshooting Guide 112

Program Challenges 112
Challenges from the Mentee Perspective 116
Challenges from the Mentor Perspective 118
Conclusion 122
Challenge Assessment 122
Self-Check: Chapter Five Review 124

Answers to Chapter Reviews 126

Chapter *One*

What is Mentoring?

Chapter Objectives

▶ Define mentoring.

▶ Understand the historical foundation of mentoring.

▶ Identify four mentor roles.

▶ Distinguish between formal and informal mentoring.

Case Study

After two years of teaching kindergarten, 25-year-old Sharon went to work for a major long-distance provider as a trainer of sales and customer service personnel. During her first few months, Sharon found the corporate environment totally foreign. Then Ron Veech became Sharon's manager. Ron recognized that although Sharon did not have a great understanding of the corporate environment, she had a tremendous potential for growth. He saw the opportunity for developing an employee who had the qualities necessary to become an exemplary member of the organization.

Ron helped Sharon develop her interpersonal skills. She learned by watching how he dealt with different situations, and he provided her many opportunities to practice. When Sharon had a particular problem to address and wanted input, she approached Ron with her ideas. She role-played what she would say, and Ron would respond accordingly. In turn, Ron would demonstrate an approach he would take, saying, "I'll show you a different way to do it," rather than "My way is better."

Ron gave Sharon room to learn, enabling her to experiment with her ideas. Sharon made mistakes, but Ron looked on those errors as a means to improve skills. Today Sharon states, "I will always remember what Ron did for me as a mentor. He really cared about me and believed in me. He helped me to expand my abilities. I was always learning."

The previous story is just one example of how mentoring is changing lives both in and out of the workplace. Mentoring programs are growing within a variety of organizations: businesses, nonprofit groups, government agencies, schools, and labor organizations. Each entity that introduces a mentoring program creates a unique approach that best suits its environment, culture, and needs. In addition to formal, structured programs, mentoring can be informal. In these instances, a mentoring relationship simply evolves as two people become closely connected in helping each other attain their personal and professional goals.

As Figure 1 illustrates, mentoring appears in many different forms and is delivered in a variety of ways depending on the degree of structure, the intent of the initiators, and the players involved.

Mentoring programs are growing within a variety of organizations.

1

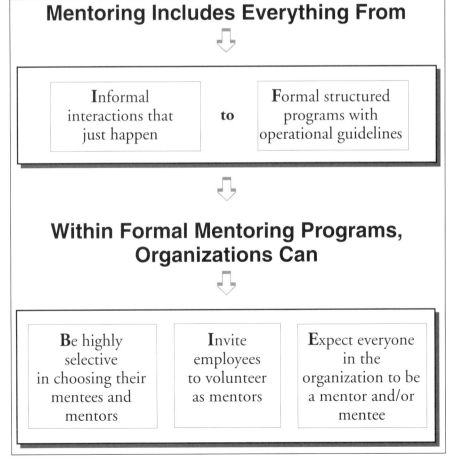

Mentoring Includes Everything From

| Informal interactions that just happen | **to** | Formal structured programs with operational guidelines |

Within Formal Mentoring Programs, Organizations Can

| Be highly selective in choosing their mentees and mentors | Invite employees to volunteer as mentors | Expect everyone in the organization to be a mentor and/or mentee |

Figure 1

Take a Moment

What do you think mentoring is? Write your own definition here.

_____

_____

_____

Defining Mentoring

In the past, mentoring was viewed as an arrangement between an older, wiser individual and a younger, less-experienced person seeking to learn and grow. The mentor would dispense his or her sage advice and, if the younger individual planned to progress in the organization, he or she would follow the advice. This kind of superior versus subordinate mentoring is currently practiced in many kinds of organizations. However, there is a movement toward a new mentoring approach: partnership. In a more collaborative approach, mentor and mentee are viewed as partners who learn from each other and establish interactions that are mutually beneficial. Their relationship is power free. It also creates an acceptable forum for managers to hear from staff about their ideas and concerns.

Some organizations are also promoting more of a peer mentoring approach. In certain situations, an employee will be a mentor because of particular skills and experiences and in another situation will switch to mentee in order to learn new skills. Peer mentoring tends to be of much shorter duration than the traditional mentoring model and can be more responsive to meeting employee needs in the constantly changing work environment of today.

> **Mentor and mentee are viewed as partners who learn from each other and establish interactions that are mutually beneficial.**

1

As you can see from the preceding descriptions, there are many different kinds of mentoring situations. However, successful mentoring relationships share some common characteristics. They are:

◆ Based on trust.

◆ Mutually beneficial.

◆ Power free.

We can use these characteristics to create a more formal definition of mentoring:

> *Mentoring* is a power-free partnership between two individuals who desire mutual growth. One of the individuals usually has greater skills, experiences, and wisdom.

Defining Related Terms

Before we progress further, we need to clarify some of the words we will use in our discussion of mentoring:

◆ *Mentor*—A close, trusted, and experienced counselor or guide.

◆ *Mentee*—One who is guided by a close, trusted, and experienced mentor.

◆ *Adviser*—One who gives advice, such as a faculty member assigned to advise students.

◆ *Advisee*—One who is advised, such as a student assigned to a faculty member for counseling.

◆ *Protégé*—A person under the care and protection of an influential person, usually for the furthering of his/her career.)

Mentor—
**A close,
trusted, and
experienced
counselor or
guide.**

When discussing the mentoring relationship in this book, we will primarily use the terms mentor and mentee because they are the most closely aligned to what we believe mentoring is all about. Using the term protégé instead of mentee implies a superior/subordinate relationship. The adviser/advisee terminology is a closer fit but doesn't capture the special relationship suggested by mentor/mentee. Using the terms adviser/advisee would be appropriate if we were discussing an educational environment only, but we are considering mentoring across a broad spectrum of organizations.

Tracing the History of Mentoring

The first mention of mentoring is in Homer's *Odyssey*, which relates the story of Odysseus' journeys and adventures. Odysseus left his son, Telemachus, under the care and protection of Mentor, who gave him guidance and advice. This arrangement was a common practice in ancient Greece as a way of maintaining the values and welfare of that civilization.

In medieval Europe, the apprenticeship system emerged. A master craftsman would take on a young, inexperienced individual with potential for growth and development and provide him the counsel and guidance he needed to learn the trade. The master craftsman mentored his apprentice and consequently ensured that the skills of his craft thrived. This apprenticeship model continues in Europe and has gained new ground in the United States in recent years with the insufficient number of skilled workers in today's workforce.

In the 1970s and early 1980s, companies began to consider mentoring programs as a way to advance employees with management potential.

Moving to more recent times, in the 1970s and early 1980s, companies began to consider mentoring programs as a way to advance employees with management potential. These programs were also seen as a strategy for providing opportunities for women and minorities, who were making the long journey to equity.

Throughout the 1990s, as many organizations adopted a team-based style of management, mentoring has taken on a new importance. In today's workplace, employees, whether managers or frontline workers, are regarded as partners. Mentoring has a natural role to play in this environment. By matching mentors with mentees, companies can bring stability, cost-effective training, and improved communication to their organizations. In addition, employee retention can result from mentoring partnerships.

So, what kinds of people are involved as mentors in today's companies? The answer is many different kinds. Being a mentor does not require a specific personality or temperament. Successful mentors do need, however, to possess several qualities that will help them work effectively with mentees.

Identifying the Qualities of a Mentor

Successful mentors share a number of important qualities. Successful mentors are:

◆ **Open minded.**
An attitude of open-mindedness is essential for the mentor/mentee relationship to blossom. A successful mentor accepts differences in culture, background, and lifestyle. A successful mentor also respects differences in communication styles and how work tasks are organized. This acceptance of diversity does not imply that expectations for the mentee's work product are low. In fact, mentors expect high quality output from their mentees.

> A successful mentor accepts differences in culture, background, and lifestyle.

◆ **Empathetic.**
Successful mentors are empathetic. They have the ability to "step into the shoes" of the mentee. If a mentor has this understanding of the mentee's position and motivation, the mentor is better able to determine what is the most appropriate strategy to use. Empathetic mentors are also patient when mentees make mistakes. Ideally, mentors encourage their mentees to be risk-takers. With risks come mistakes, and mentor patience will be tested.

◆ **Lifelong learners.**
Most mentoring programs emphasize the growth and development of the mentee. But the mentor has the opportunity to learn as well. An individual who loves to learn and continuously seeks to expand her or his horizons will look on the mentoring relationship as more than a means of transferring knowledge to a less-experienced person.

13

Successful mentors like to interact with people and enjoy close relationships.

◆ **Good communicators.**

Successful mentors like to interact with people and enjoy close relationships. They are excellent communicators. Most importantly, they listen to their mentees' needs and expectations, using the following active listening skills:

• Listening without judgment

• Clarifying to understand the speaker's intent

• Responding so communication continues

• Avoiding distractions

• Clarifying/confirming what is heard

• Reflecting feelings

• Asking for input

• Probing to uncover reasons for actions

Besides being skilled in listening, mentors are also able to clearly convey their own ideas without any "put down" or an attitude of superiority. As Stephen Covey so ably describes the key to effective communication, "seek first to understand, then to be understood."

◆ **Talented.**

Successful mentors have skills in professional work areas that benefit the mentee on the job. The mentor is willing to share the expertise gained through experience by demonstrating, modeling, and discussing skills.

◆ **Responsible.**

For mentor partnerships to succeed, mentors must take their mentoring responsibilities seriously. Mentors meet with mentees regularly, they help them set goals, and they check on their progress on a consistent basis. In turn, mentors expect mentees to exhibit responsible behavior to meet the terms of their partnership.

1

◆ **System smart.**
Good mentors know how to work within the organization. They know whom to consult for certain information, how company decisions are made, and who controls the organization's resources. A mentor has contacts throughout the system, a valuable network that mentees can use as they look for ways to learn and advance in the organization.

In programs that match mentors and mentees across different companies, the mentor's system knowledge may be of less benefit to the mentee.

The qualities we have just considered help the mentor create a partnership with the mentee. Within the mentor/mentee partnership, mentors play four primary roles that allow them to help their mentees learn and grow.

Mastering the Four Roles of a Mentor

The functions of a committed mentor are multifaceted. Each mentor has a variety of different hats to wear, depending on the situation presented by the mentee. To succeed, mentors must strengthen existing skills or develop new ones in each of these four roles:

◆ Coach

◆ Consultant

◆ Teacher

◆ Relationship-Builder

Mentor as Coach

Mentors often serve as coaches for their mentees. The primary purpose of the mentor as coach is to motivate. Consider the role of the mentor in the following example.

> **The primary purpose of the mentor as coach is to *motivate*.**

■ Jan belongs to the support staff of a claims department in a large insurance company, where she has worked for several years. Jan's department is in the midst of major change. A new manager was hired to develop and implement a team-based approach to problem solving rather than the individual-centered strategies used in the past. Jan has always managed to solve her own work-related problems. Before the changes she was excited about coming to work. Now she feels discouraged about her job. Jan's supervisor is going to serve as her mentor/coach to help her adjust to the change.

Take a Moment

If you were Jan's mentor/coach, how would you help her deal with this situation?

_____

_____

_____

_____

Jan's mentor/coach begins the coaching process by setting up a meeting with Jan. Together, the two of them work to pinpoint why Jan is discouraged. Is it because of the many changes? Is it because Jan feels her independence is being taken away? Why does Jan feel unmotivated? What personal needs are not being met by the new situation?

Once these questions have been answered, Jan's mentor/coach provides Jan with support and encouragement to address her concerns. If Jan believes that she is losing some of her personal power by having to bring issues to the team, her supervisor can help her see the advantages that can be gained by a team approach.

Jan's supervisor will continue to act as her mentor/coach until Jan is able to accept the changes she is confronting.

Mentor as Consultant

Mentors also frequently fill the role of consultant. The primary purpose of the mentor as consultant is to *identify problems* and *assist in solutions,* as illustrated in the following example:

■ John is in his mid-forties and has worked for the company since graduating from college. He has just been reassigned to a different job even though he told his manager repeatedly that he enjoyed the work he was doing. Because of his new job, John is working with an entirely different group of people, and this has been a challenge to him. One of John's teammates contradicts everything he says at the team meetings, and John feels that she keeps him from doing his job effectively. John's manager will serve as his mentor/consultant.

> The primary purpose of the mentor as consultant is to *identify problems* and *assist in solutions*.

1

Take a Moment

If you were John's mentor/consultant, how would you help him deal with this situation?

_____

_____

_____

_____

John's mentor/consultant talks with John to help him identify his problem or problems. Is it a change in work environment? Is it the demands of the new job? Is it because he is uncomfortable working with different people? Is it because of the effect his teammate's behavior has on him?

Once the problem is identified, John and his mentor/consultant work to determine its root cause. For example, is the teammate contradicting John, or does he just feel vulnerable because he is new? Does John present underdeveloped ideas to the team, which causes a negative reaction from his teammate? Is the teammate feeling threatened by John's ability?

Once they have determined the root cause of the problem, the mentor/consultant can help John brainstorm a list of possible strategies, choose the most appropriate, and create a plan of action.

Mentor as Teacher

> **The primary purpose of the mentor as teacher is to *assist in skill and competency development.***

Mentors often serve as teachers for their mentees. The primary purpose of the mentor as teacher is to *assist in skill and competency development.* This is illustrated in the following example:

■ Michael is a new hire and recent college graduate. He was excited by the offer to work for a large state bank and was enthused about starting work. Unfortunately, once he started working, he discovered that he was lacking some of the key computer skills he needed to do an excellent job. In order for Michael to succeed, he needs help with developing specific skills for his job. Michael's coworker will serve as his mentor/teacher.

Take a Moment

If you were Michael's mentor/teacher, how would you help him deal with this situation?

_____

_____

_____

_____

Michael's mentor/teacher begins by meeting with Michael to identify his learning needs. Together, they determine what specific computer skills he lacks. Michael and his mentor/teacher next discuss possible options. Does the mentor have sufficient skills to help him? Should Michael attend a class? Are there any videos or training materials available to help him develop his skills?

After Michael receives training, he continues to practice his computer skills. He demonstrates his new skills for his mentor/teacher and asks for feedback.

Mentor as Relationship-Builder

The fourth role that mentors serve for their mentees is as relationship-builders. The primary purpose of the mentor as relationship builder is to *facilitate the management of relationships.* Consider the following example.

■ Kim has always had a problem "connecting" with her supervisor. Kim is very creative and often comes up with ideas for a new product embellishment. Unfortunately, she tends to be late for meetings and to spend a good portion of her day "socializing" with other employees in the office. Kim's supervisor, on the other hand, is very structured and formal in his approach. He expects deadlines to be met, appointments to be kept, and actions to be "by the book." Kim has asked a coworker from another department to serve as her mentor/relationship-builder.

> The primary purpose of the mentor as relationship-builder is to *facilitate the management of relationships.*

Take a Moment

If you were Kim's mentor/relationship-builder, how would you help her deal with this situation?

_____

_____

_____

_____

Kim's mentor/relationship-builder begins by listening carefully to Kim's perception of her relationship with her supervisor. The mentor points out to Kim the different behavioral styles that she and her supervisor use. Kim accomplishes her tasks through her interactions with others using an unstructured approach. Her supervisor, on the other hand, has a more formal style and follows a prescribed series of steps to do his job.

The mentor and Kim discuss the value of diversity, and the mentor asks Kim for suggestions on what strategies to use with her supervisor that would improve communication. The mentor emphasizes how differences enrich the workplace and how Kim can adapt her communication style to be more systematic and formal to match the style of her supervisor.

Mentors must be skilled in the four mentor roles of coach, consultant, teacher, and relationship-builder, so that they can select the role that will most appropriately meet the needs of the mentee. The following chapter delves into each of the four roles to clarify the particular skills needed as a mentor. It helps a mentor assess his/her level of skill and provides step-by-step guides on how to successfully fill the four mentor roles.

Chapter Summary

Today, mentoring programs are growing within a variety of organizations, including businesses, nonprofit groups, government agencies, schools, and labor organizations. Within these diverse organizations, mentoring can take a variety of forms and may take place as part of formal, structured programs or informal relationships that evolve on their own.

Though there are many different kinds of mentoring situations, successful mentoring relationships share some common characteristics. They are:

◆ Based on trust.

◆ Mutually beneficial.

◆ Power free.

We can define mentoring as a *power-free partnership between two individuals who desire mutual growth. One of the individuals usually has greater skills, experiences, and wisdom.*

Though there is no one type of person who is best suited to be a mentor, successful mentors share a number of qualities. Successful mentors are:

◆ Open minded.

◆ Empathetic.

◆ Lifelong learners.

◆ Good communicators.

◆ Talented.

◆ Responsible.

◆ System smart.

These qualities can help the mentor build a partnership with the mentee that will create learning and growth opportunities for both parties. As this partnership develops, the mentor will take on four major roles when working with the mentee. These roles are:

◆ **Coach**—Encouraging the mentee to remain motivated.

◆ **Consultant**—Helping the mentee identify problems and assisting in their solution.

◆ **Teacher**—Assisting the mentee in skill and competency development.

◆ **Relationship-Builder**—Facilitating the management of relationships.

Mentors choose the roles they will play based on mentee needs.

Self-Check: Chapter One Review

Answers appear on page 126.

1. What are three characteristics that make a mentoring relationship unique?

   a. _____

   b. _____

   c. _____

2. What are the four mentor roles?

   a. _____

   b. _____

   c. _____

   d. _____

3. What seven personal qualities are common to successful mentors?

   a. _____

   b. _____

   c. _____

   d. _____

   e. _____

   f. _____

   g. _____

4. What distinguishes formal from informal mentoring?

   A formal program _____

   _____

   An informal program _____

   _____

Notes

Chapter *Two*

Identifying Mentor Roles and Skills

Chapter Objectives

▶ Identify the roles that you most need to learn about and practice to be a successful mentor.

▶ Define the four roles of a mentor.

▶ Identify the characteristics and skills needed for a mentor as coach, consultant, teacher, and relationship-builder.

Case Study

Janet has been involved with mentoring as both a mentor and a mentee for the past 20 years. After leaving a teaching position, she worked for a utility company as an area office clerk and later as a collections clerk. In these positions, Janet learned to separate herself from an environment that she describes as supporting "favoritism and discrimination." Females staffed most of the clerical jobs, and males were in marketing or management. After Janet was passed over for a promotion, she began volunteering for special projects. As a result, she was offered greater job responsibilities until she became a regional representative for the company.

At this point, mentoring became a real part of Janet's life. Her supervisor served as her first mentor, helping her acquire the technical skills required for her position. When she became an area manager, Janet learned even more from the people she supervised. "Some of the best mentors were the employees who worked for me," Janet recalls. "I was fortunate to have linemen who would take the time to show me how something worked."

Since those days, Janet has used what she learned as a mentee to mentor both women and men as they work to advance their careers. The last person that Janet mentored before leaving the utility company was a young man just out of college. Janet and the young man jointly created his development plan. Janet gave him advice when he asked for it and put him in touch with those in the company who could help him. "This understanding of the network is just as important as developing the technical skills of the business," states Janet.

2

As we have seen, mentors play a variety of roles when working with their mentees, and they need to develop a number of qualities in order to play those roles effectively. Do you have the skills necessary to be a mentor? Take a moment now to review the roles of a mentor and the skills needed to successfully perform them. Are there areas in which you need to improve?

Mentoring Self-Assessment

Mentor as Coach (to motivate)

	Always	Sometimes	Never
1. I like to get people excited about their jobs.	2	1	0
2. When a mentee does not yet meet my expectations but has improved his/her performance, I give positive reinforcement.	2	1	0
3. I avoid those people who are negative about their jobs and coworkers.	2	1	0
4. I believe everyone can achieve success.	2	1	0

Mentor as Consultant (to help identify problems and develop strategies to address them)

	Always	Sometimes	Never
1. I have good analytical skills that help me get to the root of a problem.	2	1	0

	Always	Sometimes	Never
2. I think people need to seek their own solutions to problems.	2	1	0
3. Sometimes you have to take a risk and try something even if it hasn't proved effective yet.	2	1	0
4. I can see how all the parts of a situation interrelate and contribute to the "big" picture.	2	1	0

Mentor as Teacher (to assist in skill and competency development)

	Always	Sometimes	Never
1. I have patience in helping others develop their skills.	2	1	0
2. I recognize that adult learners have distinct needs.	2	1	0
3. Measuring skill development is crucial for personal development.	2	1	0
4. I believe that everyone can learn.	2	1	0

Mentor as Relationship-Builder (to facilitate the management of relationships)

	Always	Sometimes	Never
1. I am an active listener.	2	1	0
2. I see conflict as a win/win situation.	2	1	0
3. When people have problems, I help them clarify their thoughts without telling them what to do.	2	1	0
4. A diverse workplace makes for a rich mix of perspectives that benefits the organization.	2	1	0

Record your scores below. The higher the score, the higher the degree of skill you possess.

Mentor as Coach Score   _____

Mentor as Consultant Score   _____

Mentor as Teacher Score   _____

Mentor as Relationship-Builder Score   _____

Total Score (32 possible)   _____

Where I am the most skilled   _____

Where I need the most development   _____

In the following sections, you will learn about the most important skills needed in the four mentor roles of coach, consultant, teacher, and relationship-builder.

2

Developing the Skills of a Coach

How did you rate your coaching ability? As a motivator, the coach needs the following skills.

Skill 1: Ability to Project Enthusiasm

As a coach you must let your mentee know that you believe he or she will succeed. You are the cheerleader—the person who gives encouragement and support. The enthusiasm you show will energize your mentee to achieve more than she or he ever imagined possible. You create a climate in which your mentee is excited and willing to try new strategies without fear of failure.

> As a coach, you must let your mentee know that you believe he or she will succeed.

Skill 2: Ability to Motivate

You must determine what motivates your mentee. Each person's drive is different. Some people are driven by a need to achieve, others value relationships, some need recognition, and others seek security. You must recognize that what motivates you may be quite different than what motivates your mentee.

According to a 1995 study by Kenneth Kovack of George Mason University, supervisors are often unaware of what truly motivates their employees. In the study, supervisors placed *good wages, job security,* and *promotion and growth* as the top three strategies that they believed would motivate their employees. However, the employees stated that *interesting work, full appreciation of the work done* and a *feeling of being in on things* were their primary motivators.

Dr. Abraham Maslow's Hierarchy of Needs, a classic theory of motivation, can help mentors recognize what factors motivate their mentees. Maslow's Hierarchy organizes needs into five different levels:

◆ Physiological needs (air, food, water, and sex)

◆ Safety needs (shelter, safety, and security)

◆ Social needs (personal relationships)

◆ Esteem needs (recognition)

◆ Self-Actualization (the opportunity to realize one's full potential)

As figure 2 illustrates, first-level needs must be met before someone can be motivated by higher-level needs. In other words, if the basic need for food is not being met, other factors, such as safety and self-esteem, are of lesser immediate consequence. The need for food has to be satisfied before other higher-level needs will create a motivating drive.

2

> **Maslow's Hierarchy organizes needs into five different levels.**

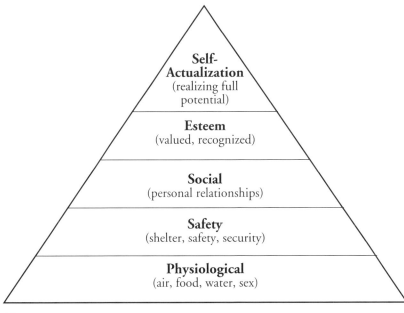

Figure 2

Maslow's Heirarchy of Needs is an excellent tool for helping mentors to recognize what factors motivate their mentees. To apply Maslow's Hierarchy to a mentoring situation, we can see that if a mentee is concerned about losing his or her job (safety), developing personal relationships and gaining recognition will not be motivators. Mentors need to seek out what particular mentee needs prevail and use strategies based on those motivational forces. Simply listening to your mentee is a good way to identify his or her motivators.

Skill 3: Ability to Give Constructive Feedback

As an effective coach, you need to be highly skilled in giving feedback. You must learn to be honest, whether you are praising your mentee for a job well done or suggesting areas for improvement. Feedback must be constructive, a means to help the other individual grow and learn.

Feedback must be constructive, a means to help the other individual grow and learn.

When you give feedback:

◆ Choose the time and place so that your mentee feels at ease.

◆ Remember to provide positive feedback as well as corrective feedback.

◆ Help your mentee accept praise.

◆ Give specific examples to illustrate particular behaviors that you wish to reinforce or correct.

◆ Don't rely on hearsay or other people's opinions.

A feedback frequently used in sports coaching is called the positive sandwich. To make a *positive sandwich*, begin your comments with praise for an action that was commendable. Then move to an instruction regarding behavior you would like to see change in the future, such as "If you speak openly to your supervisor about your concern, you will feel more comfortable about working collaboratively in the future." Next, conclude with a positive statement of support. This approach uses two positive comments wrapped around some instruction.

Effective sports coaches also use positive reinforcement rather than negative criticism to help athletes improve performance. Rewarding positive behaviors increases the likelihood of the behaviors being repeated and contributes to an environment that is both pleasant and promotes growth. At the same time, effective coaches regard mistakes as opportunities for learning rather than for criticism.

2

Take a Moment

Think about a time when you received criticism for a particular behavior. How did you feel?

_____

Now think about an occasion when you were given positive reinforcement for a certain behavior. How did you feel?

_____

Were you more motivated to improve performance by criticism or positive reinforcement?

_____

A mentor/coach uses enthusiasm, knowledge of individual motivation, and superior feedback skills to motivate the mentee to take risks, learn from mistakes, and continually make personal improvements.

Developing the Skills of a Consultant

Do you feel comfortable in your role as a consultant? To help mentees identify and solve problems, the consultant needs the following skills.

Skill 1: Ability to Enable Problem Solving

According to Chip R. Bell, author of *Managers as Mentors,* a major trap for mentors is saying to a mentee, "I can help." The mentor's job is to facilitate learning and not to tell the mentee what to do. The goal of the mentoring partnership is for the mentee to arrive at a solution. Mentors might share with their mentees similar situations that they have encountered and what strategies they have used, but this is simply to provide the mentees with additional information to use in making a decision. The mentor's priorities are to be a listener and to help the mentee follow an effective decision-making process.

> The goal of the mentoring partnership is for the mentee to arrive at a solution.

Skill 2: Ability to Follow the Problem-Solving Process

In order to guide mentees through the problem-solving process, mentors must be familiar with that process themselves. Problem solving can be broken down into an easy-to-follow six-step process:

Step 1: Define the Problem
The first step in any problem-solving situation is to accurately identify the problem. Sometimes a problem is obvious, as when a machine breaks down and must be repaired before work can continue. But in many other situations, the problem is not clear cut. What appears to be the problem may only be the symptom of a deeper root cause that is in fact the real problem. The following example of a worker not receiving messages illustrates how asking a series of questions can help define the root cause of a problem.

Questions	Answers
1. What do you believe is the problem?	Mary does not pass on my messages in a timely manner, and some of my clients are angry about the slow response.
2. What are possible causes of the problem?	• Mary doesn't have the time to see that I receive my messages. • Mary doesn't like me. • Mary doesn't understand how important it is for me to get my messages.
3. What can you do to collect additional information to clarify the root cause?	• Talk to Mary. • Examine the process for passing on messages. • Talk to the other receptionists to see how they convey messages in a timely fashion.
4. What is the real problem?	Mary does not have a systematic way of passing on messages.

Mentors can ask mentees questions to help them define their problem. Mentors should encourage mentees to keep searching until they find the root cause of any problem situation.

Step 2: Brainstorm Ideas
Try to come up as many ways to address the problem as possible. Don't worry about judging the feasibility of the solutions-that will come later. Instead, encourage creativity and thinking outside the box. Encourage mentees to generate outrageous, diverse ideas. The craziest thoughts often produce the sanest solutions to problems!

Try to come up as many ways to address the problem as possible.

33

Step 3: Prioritize Ideas

Once you've brainstormed ideas, you can prioritize them as possible solutions to the problem. First, develop a set of criteria for selection purposes. Measuring each idea against a consistent set of criteria will help you select the most suitable idea for addressing the problem.

Possible criteria for evaluating solutions to the "Mary situation" described earlier might include:

◆ Disrupts the least number of employees.

◆ Is low cost.

◆ Is acceptable to other team members.

◆ Provides a long-term solution.

Mentors should never choose solutions for their mentees.

Mentors should never choose solutions for their mentees. Instead, they should help mentees generate useful criteria and then encourage the mentees to use the criteria to carefully evaluate their solutions.

Step 4: Develop an Action Plan

Once you've selected the most appropriate solution, develop a plan of action to address the problem situation. Ask the questions What? When? and How? and consider what resources you will use and how you will measure your results, as in the following example.

Action Plan
WHAT are you going to do?
WHEN are you going to do it?
HOW are you going to do it?

WHAT RESOURCES do you need to complete this action?
WHAT MEASURES will you use?

2

If we return to the problem with Mary, the Action Plan might look like this.

Action Plan

WHAT?
Meet with Mary

WHEN?
Tomorrow

HOW?
Invite Mary to have coffee in the cafeteria to discuss how messages are handled.

RESOURCES?
Time to meet, strategize, test out ideas, and measure effectiveness of changes.

MEASURES?
Mary will deliver messages within 10 minutes of their arrival.

Step 5 Implementation
An action plan can only be effective if it is carried out. At this stage in the problem-solving process, mentors can use coaching skills to encourage and support mentees as they deal with a problem area. Setting up a time to meet to discuss the situation following an action will be beneficial to the mentee. During this meeting, the mentee can share events that occurred and determine whether appropriate action was taken. The mentor's primary task is to listen and to provide feedback and encouragement as needed.

Mentors can use coaching skills to encourage and support mentees as they deal with a problem area.

35

Step 6: Evaluation

Was the solution successful? What worked? What could be done differently next time? The mentor should guide the mentee towards evaluating the success of the action. The question, "Did the action have the desired results?" has to be repeatedly answered in order to evaluate the effectiveness of the action and to make any necessary changes for improvement.

> **As a mentor, the role of consultant to the mentee is one of collaboration rather than one of expert to novice.**

As a mentor, the role of consultant to the mentee is one of collaboration rather than one of expert to novice. The emphasis should be on the problem-solving process and on empowering the mentee to confront an issue and to make decisions about what actions to take.

Developing the Skills of a Teacher

How did you rate your skills as a teacher? To assist mentees in their skill and competency development, the consultant needs the following skills:

Skill 1: Ability to Adapt to Adult Learners

> **In their role as teacher, mentors also need to understand characteristics of the adult learner.**

We already know that mentors must be lifelong learners. In their role as teacher they also need to understand characteristics of the adult learner. In order to be effective, information designed for adult learners should be:

◆ **Problem centered.**
Adults want to learn about how to deal with the problems they face. They want to know how they will benefit from the learning experience. Learning has to be worth their time.

◆ **Experiential.**
Adults prefer hands-on experiential learning activities rather than a straight lecture format. The learning becomes more meaningful when there is active rather than passive involvement.

◆ **Applicable.**
Adults want to apply what they learn to their own situations. The learning needs to be both relevant and timely.

◆ **Self-directed.**
Adults tend to be self-directed in their learning. However, if their only educational experience came about by sitting back and passively listening to an "expert" teacher, they might wait to be directed in their learning activities. Most adults, however, prefer teachers who are supportive rather than directive.

2

◆ **Internally motivated.**
Adults tend to be motivated to learn when something interests them or impacts their work rather than by extrinsic factors, such as grades or certificates.

◆ **Experience based.**
Adults come to the learning situation with many experiences and skills already developed. The mentor as teacher must help the learner use these experiences and skills as a bridge to new learning opportunities.

Take a Moment

1. Think of a situation in which you tried to help someone improve competence in a certain area:

   Who? _____

   What Skill? _____

2. What did you do to encourage that individual to learn?

   _____

   _____

   _____

3. How did you know the skill had been improved?

   _____

   _____

   _____

Skill 2: Ability to Use a Skill-Development Process

An effective way for mentors in the teacher role to help employees learn is to use a sequential skill-development process.

Step 1: Assess Learning Needs

In order to determine which skills to develop, the mentor and mentee must first identify the greatest area of need. Also, they must determine the gap between the current skill level and the desired skill level regarding a specific set of competencies. The mentee will probably be aware of the skill areas that require development, but if confirmation is needed, a competency matrix can be helpful. The mentee should list all the competencies for the job and rate the skill level on each competency to determine the skills needing the most development. A competency list for a Program Coordinator might look like this:

> **In order to determine which skills to develop, the mentor and mentee must first identify the greatest area of need.**

Job Position: Program Coordinator

Excellent = **5** Very Good = **4** Good = **3** Fair = **2** Poor = **1**

Competencies

1.	Working with others	5 4 3 2 1
2.	Managing time	5 4 3 2 1
3.	Being a creative problem-solver	5 4 3 2 1
4.	Giving attention to detail	5 4 3 2 1
5.	Organizing activities	5 4 3 2 1
6.	Delegating	5 4 3 2 1
7.	Working with committees	5 4 3 2 1
8.	Making decisions	5 4 3 2 1
9.	Managing budgets	5 4 3 2 1

The mentee will rate skill level and see those areas that need the most development. Observing the mentee at work will also help the mentor view first-hand what the mentee does well and what should be targeted for improvement.

Step 2: Discuss Options

Once the priority skill areas have been identified, the mentor and mentee should brainstorm approaches for skill development.

Possible strategies for developing skills might include:

◆ Observing the mentor at work.

◆ Observing another employee.

◆ Watching a video.

◆ Attending a class.

◆ Working with a more skilled partner.

◆ Reading instructional material.

◆ Seeking opportunities to practice.

◆ Networking with employees from other companies.

◆ Attending professional association meetings and training seminars.

2

Step 3: Select an Approach

At this point, the mentor and mentee should agree on an action plan and put it in writing. The mentor and mentee need to agree on what actions will be taken, when and how they will occur, the resources needed, and how the effectiveness of the actions will be measured, as in the following example:

> **The mentor and mentee should agree on an action plan and put it in writing.**

Action Plan
WHAT? Handle customer complaints without getting angry
WHEN? Immediately
HOW? • Observe mentor handling calls for customers • Watch video
RESOURCES? • Time for mentee to observe • Video
MEASURES? Has the percentage of angry responses decreased?

Step 4: Implement

The next step is to implement the action plan by helping the mentee develop the necessary skills. The following process can be especially useful for skill development:

◆ **Demonstrate**
The mentor demonstrates the competency at a highly skilled level or assigns another individual with skill in that particular area to do the demonstration. In addition, videos, computer-based training, the Internet, and internal and external training sessions can all provide valuable demonstrations of skills being used effectively.

◆ **Observe**
The mentee observes the demonstrated behavior. The mentee notes the difference between his or her own normal behavior and the demonstrated level of skill.

◆ **Practice**
Next comes practice. The mentor and mentee might have the opportunity to use the skill as a team. This is an ideal way for the mentee to practice with the support of the mentor as a backup. Once the mentee has gained confidence, then he or she can use the skill in a solo capacity.

The key here is practice, practice, and more practice.

◆ **Feedback**
The mentor's role as teacher is to provide constructive feedback. (Please see page 30 for specifics about giving feedback.) In response to the feedback, the mentee should practice, demonstrate, and again receive feedback so that the skill can be continuously improved.

The Demonstrate, Observe, Feedback process should be repeated as needed for the mentee to acquire the targeted skill. A good measure of whether a skill has been adopted is when that skill is used in a different arena. Transference from one situation to another indicates that learning has occurred.

Videos, computer-based training, the Internet, and internal and external training sessions can all provide valuable demonstrations of skills being used effectively.

Step 5: Verify Accomplishments

Determining whether the mentee's actions have been successful is crucial. Remember that measurements for determining the effectiveness of the actions were included in the action plan.

One effective system for evaluating a mentee's actions is the Evaluation Model developed by Donald Kirkpatrick. He stated that there are four levels at which evaluation of training can occur:

◆ **Level 1: Reaction**

This measures the *satisfaction* of the client or customer. In the mentor/mentee relationship, we would measure how satisfied the mentee feels with the training received.

◆ **Level 2: Learning**

This measures whether there have been any changes in *attitudes, skills,* or *knowledge* as a result of the training. At this level, the measure would be to determine whether the mentee has changed skills, attitudes, or knowledge after working with the mentor/teacher.

◆ **Level 3: Behavior**

This measures any *changes in behavior* because of the training. The mentee would demonstrate different behaviors on the job because of the teaching strategies of the mentor/teacher.

◆ **Level 4 : Results**

This measures whether there are any *concrete results* because of the training. Included could be improved production, lower costs, increased sales, or reduced turnover of employees. It may be difficult to isolate the impact of the mentor's teaching skill from other factors in the work situation that could have influenced the results.

The mentor as teacher ultimately wants to help the mentee develop skills that will positively impact the organization. The mentor discusses with the mentee the career opportunities that could open up, both internal and external to the organization, as a result of the improved skill development.

2

> Determining whether the mentee's actions have been successful is crucial.

The mentee will also gain many additional personal benefits. Not only will the job tasks become easier, but there will certainly be an increase in motivation to learn more highly developed skills. The mentee will be recognized within the company as a valued employee and the mentee's self-esteem will receive a boost.

Developing the Skills of a Relationship-Builder

Finally, how do you feel about your skills as a relationship-builder? To help mentees with the management of relationships, the mentor needs the following skills:

Skill 1: Ability to Listen Effectively

A mentor must have excellent listening skills.

A mentor must have excellent listening skills. Those skills include the ability to listen not only to the content of what is being said but also to the emotions that are being expressed. By paying attention to a speaker's tone of voice, body language, and facial expressions, a good listener can detect such emotions as anger, frustration, fear, and confusion that a speaker might not be comfortable expressing verbally.

There are a variety of strategies that, in this mentor role, can be an aid to active listening. These techniques indicate to the mentee that what is being said is of value and is important to the mentor.

◆ **Acknowledging** says to the mentee, "I am listening to what you have to say." This can be done by nodding, saying "um" or "aha," and by using facial expressions to indicate interest. Leaning toward the mentee, keeping eye contact, and not being distracted are all ways of showing you care about what is being said.

◆ **Using silence** says to the mentee, "What you have to say is important." Often, a "helper," in this case, the mentor, feels the urge to jump in and direct the conversation or give advice before the whole story has been told. This interrupts the flow and causes the discussion to be sidetracked. By being silent—yet still acknowledging interest through body language and facial expressions—the mentor can effectively say, "I am interested in what you are saying."

◆ **Clarifying** says to the mentee, "I want to know more." Clarifying is accomplished by asking open-ended questions, such as, "Could you tell me what you meant when you said Jean misunderstood you?" "What are you referring to?" and "What are you hoping to do?" These are questions that require a response beyond a "yes" or "no." They ask for more information. This indicates interest and extends support to the mentee.

2

◆ **Paraphrasing** says to the mentee, "I understand what you are saying." This technique involves restating in your own words what you think the mentee said. The mentor might say, "I think I'm hearing you say that when you approached John about the communication problem, he implied that he didn't have time to deal with it." Once the mentee has confirmed that what you said is correct or modifies it to be accurate, the conversation can continue.

> **Paraphrasing says to the mentee, "I understand what you are saying."**

◆ **Reflecting** says to the mentee, "I understand what you are feeling." This technique delves beyond paraphrasing, which deals with the content of what the mentee says, to identify what the mentee is actually feeling. The mentee might say, "I can't believe Sue got a promotion and I didn't." The mentor might respond, "You sound pretty disappointed," which goes beyond the content (not getting a promotion) to the feeling that the mentee is experiencing (disappointed).

◆ **Summarizing** says to the mentee, "This is what the situation seems to be." The mentor summarizes the main elements of the conversation and asks the mentee for confirmation. This ensures that the mentor fully understands the mentee's point of view.

Take a Moment

How do you rate yourself on your active listening skills?

	Highly Skilled		Need Improvement		Low Skilled
Using Silence	5	4	3	2	1
Clarifying	5	4	3	2	1
Paraphrasing	5	4	3	2	1
Reflecting	5	4	3	2	1
Summarizing	5	4	3	2	1

Not only must a mentor as relationship-builder be an effective listener, he/she must also know how to manage conflict wisely.

Skill 2: Knowledge of Conflict Management

As a relationship-builder, you must be well grounded in conflict management skills in order to help mentees deal with the conflicts they are bound to encounter. What is your own view of conflict? Respond to the following statements; then read the explanations that follow.

1.	Conflict is bad	True	False
2.	Conflict creates winners and losers.	True	False
3.	Offices in which there is a lot of conflict are poorly managed.	True	False
4.	Most people don't like dealing with conflict.	True	False
5.	Most conflicts can be managed.	True	False

1. **Conflict is bad.**
   We may feel uncomfortable, vulnerable, and fearful when faced with conflict, but we should not look on conflict as bad. Instead, we should regard conflict positively. It is an opportunity to open up communication and to deal with the issues that are important to us.

> **Conflict is an opportunity to open up communication and to deal with the issues that are important to us.**

2. **Conflict creates winners and losers.**
   Our goal should be to use conflict to constructively create solutions that all players can agree to support. Not everyone has to agree 100 percent, but everyone has to stand behind the decision once it is made. Individuals are not perceived as winners and losers, which would reinforce the rift between the two points of view, but as collaborators joining their abilities to find workable solutions.

3. **Lots of conflict means poor leadership.**
   Conflict occurs everywhere; it is a fact of life. Lots of conflict can result in a creative, highly energized workforce. On the other hand, it can waste time, sap energy, and be

counterproductive. The key is in how well the conflict is managed by those in leadership positions.

4. **Most people dislike conflict.**
   We would all like to live in a world that is peaceful and harmonious, but that is not reality. Most people find conflict stressful, but many of these same people also come to enjoy the challenge that comes from resolving conflict successfully. Some people even learn to embrace conflict as a means for personal growth. Everyone has a choice about handling conflict.

5. **Most conflicts can be managed.**
   As you might have guessed from the previous points, conflict can be managed so that all sides involved come out as winners. The following steps can help you manage conflict successfully.

> Conflict can be managed so that all sides involved come out as winners.

Steps for Managing Conflict Constructively

Before the Meeting

Step 1: Create an Acceptable Environment
Consider such issues as:

- **Location**—Select a neutral, private place where both parties can speak freely and neither has home advantage.

- **Timing**—Schedule the meeting at a time convenient to and agreeable to both parties. Allow enough time to enable some progress to be made.

- **Invitation**—The invitation to meet should be phrased in terms of collaborating to find a viable solution.

During the Meeting

Step 2: Clarify the Situation

- **Listen to both sides of the story.**
  Representatives of both parties must explain their perceptions of the situation.

2

Often conflict can be addressed at this level because there is simply a misunderstanding about what was said. One person meant something in particular and the recipient of the message interpreted it incorrectly.

♦ **Gather information.**
Ensure that all the information is available for discussion. Ask questions such as "Who is involved?" "What happened?" "When did it happen?" "Where did it occur?" and "Why do you think it happened?"

♦ **Identify the issue.**
Focus on the real issue without getting sidetracked by other facts or concerns. Discuss what each party needs (rather than wants) in the conflict situation. (For example, I want my questions to be answered within an hour; I need my questions to be answered within 24 hours so that I can respond to customers.)

Focus on the real issue without getting sidetracked by other facts or concerns.

Step 3: Generate Options

♦ Put as many ideas forward as can be generated. At this stage, any ideas can be viewed as possibilities.

♦ Examine each of the ideas to determine how feasible they are and whether they meet the needs of both parties. Ask, "If this strategy is adopted, what is the projected outcome?"

♦ Look for common areas of interest where agreement is more likely to be reached.

Step 4: Select an Option

♦ Sometimes rushing to a solution eliminates the opportunity to find a better approach. Be sure that any option you choose isn't just a quick fix.

♦ Determine that the option chosen can be accomplished with the resources available.

♦ Again, select an option that will best meet the needs of both parties.

After the Meeting

Step 5: Implement

◆ Try the chosen approach.

◆ Arrange for both parties to meet to discuss progress.

Step 6: Review

◆ Meet to verify that the option agreed upon is being implemented and is working.

◆ Discuss possible ways to improve the arrangement.

Chapter Summary

Mentors need a variety of skills to play the roles of coach, consultant, teacher, and relationship-builder.

◆ To succeed as a coach, a mentor needs these skills:

　1. Ability to project enthusiasm

　2. Ability to motivate

　3. Ability to give constructive feedback

◆ To succeed as a consultant, a mentor needs these skills:

　1. Ability to enable problem solving

　2. Ability to follow the problem-solving process

◆ To succeed as a teacher, a mentor needs these skills:

　1. Ability to adapt to adult learners

　2. Ability to use a skill-development process

◆ To succeed as a relationship-builder, a mentor needs these skills:

　1. Ability to listen effectively

　2. Ability to manage conflict effectively

Self-Check: Chapter Two Review

Answers appear on page 126 and 127.

1. True or False?
   To be an effective mentor, you need to play multiple roles.

2. List three skills a successful mentor/coach needs to succeed:

   a. _____

   b. _____

   c. _____

3. What are six steps to take in problem solving?

   a. _____

   b. _____

   c. _____

   d. _____

   e. _____

   f. _____

4. Name six characteristics of information designed for the adult learner.

   a. _____

   b. _____

   c. _____

   d. _____

   e. _____

   f. _____

5. True or False?
   Silence is a legitimate strategy to use as a mentor in the role of relationship-builder.

Notes

2

Chapter*Three*

Creating a Formal Mentoring Program

Chapter Objectives

▶ Identify different mentoring approaches.

▶ Recognize the organizational benefits and challenges of mentoring.

▶ Recognize the personal benefits and challenges of mentoring.

▶ Explain the steps for creating a mentoring program.

▶ Develop mentoring program guidelines.

Case Study

At the age of 14, a young man was at a crossroads in his life. He was on the fringes of a gang, he was experimenting with drugs, and he kind of liked football. His mother realized he needed some positive direction and got him involved in a Big Brothers/Big Sisters program.

After being matched for four years, he graduated from high school with an all-state football award and grades good enough for his name to appear on the honor roll. He received a football scholarship and is now attending college.

This young man recently contacted the Big Brothers/Big Sisters program near his college. He wants to be a Big Brother—to help someone in the same way that he was helped. "Truly, we have no idea when we touch the life of one young person how many people will be touched by the ripple effect," states Althea Holcomb, Executive Director of Big Brothers/Big Sisters of Greater Des Moines, Iowa.

Mentoring can take place in many settings and incorporate many styles. If you recall from Chapter One, mentoring can range from "informal interactions that just happen" to "formal structured programs with operational guidelines." Informal mentoring relationships are nearly always successful. Those developed formally provide more of a challenge.

Identifying the Characteristics of Formal Mentoring Programs

The goal of any formal mentoring program is to create an environment in which mentoring can flourish. Formal programs, however, may differ widely in the approach and delivery of mentoring. Consider the different ways in which mentors and mentees may be chosen:

> The goal of any formal mentoring program is to create an environment in which mentoring can flourish.

3

1. **Selective programs**
   Formal programs can be highly selective when choosing their mentees and mentors. This approach is taken when individuals are targeted as mentees because they have potential for advancement or they need special support. Mentors are matched to mentees because of their strengths and skills in areas where the mentee seeks development. This strategy has been used to advance women, minorities, and potential managers through the ranks and to increase retention in entry-level positions. Mentors and mentees are carefully screened and matched in this approach.

2. **Volunteer programs**
   In some programs, anyone who wants to provide assistance to a fellow employee with less experience can sign up to be a mentor. The mentor's involvement, although fully supported by the organization, is totally voluntary. In this type of program, the organizers need to carefully examine mentee needs and to match that person with a mentor who has greater skills and experience in identified areas of need.

3. **All-organization programs**
   This approach identifies mentoring relationships as an inherent part of the organizational culture. Employees are expected to seize opportunities to mentor new employees and those they feel will benefit from their advanced skills. Management models appropriate behavior by mentoring less-

experienced employees in the organization. Mentoring becomes an organizational mindset. In this kind of culture, peer mentoring (helping colleagues who need skill development in your area of expertise) and team mentoring (pooling resources by individuals to benefit other team members) flourish.

Take a Moment

Have you had experience with any of these types of mentoring programs? Was the program effective for you?

Designing and Proposing a Program

No matter what type of mentoring program you wish to build, you can begin to develop it by following these steps.

Step 1: Determine the Purpose

An organization that is starting to develop mentoring relationships must first determine the program's purpose—what it is hoping to achieve.

An organization that wishes to develop mentoring relationships must first determine the program's purpose—what it is hoping to achieve. Responding to the following questions will help clarify the project expectations.

❑ Are you hoping to advance a targeted population within your company, such as members of minority groups, entry-level employees, or new managers?

❑ Are you seeking a way to help newcomers acclimate to the organization?

❑ Is this program intended to help employees build skills?

❑ Is this program intended to bring about culture change?

❑ Is this program intended to assist employees in their career development by using mentoring as a vehicle for networking with key company people?

❑ Do you want to create connections between employees to provide stability in a time of great change?

❑ Are you seeking ways to increase job retention?

At this point, to clarify the purpose of mentoring for the organization and to build commitment to the project, encourage a group of individuals who represent a cross section of the company to meet and discuss the merits of mentoring. This group can conduct a survey within the organization in order to:

♦ Determine whether the culture is ready to accept and support mentoring.

♦ Identify the greatest needs for mentoring.

♦ Pinpoint potential barriers that could negatively impact a mentoring initiative.

3

These people can then be the emissaries who spread the word about the initiative throughout the organization. As they interact with members of the organization, this group can also bring back ideas to the program designers and provide feedback from the field on how the initiative is being received.

Step 2: Seek Organizational Commitment

Once you determine the purpose of your mentoring program, you should begin:

♦ Gathering data.

♦ Researching successful mentoring programs (see Chapter 4).

♦ Building a case for investing time, energy, and financial resources into the project.

Use the information you find to build an argument promoting mentoring as a viable strategy for organizational development. Also share with decision makers specific benefits and challenges of mentoring (listed in the following tables) and the impact they can have on the organization. Using an honest approach at the beginning of the enterprise will help you ensure that no surprises will occur to destroy your efforts.

Use the information you find to build an argument promoting mentoring as a viable strategy for organizational development.

Organizational Benefits and Challenges of Mentoring

<u>Benefits of Mentoring</u>	<u>Challenges of Mentoring</u>

Healthy Work Environment

- Helps support the organizational mission

- Encourages creative ideas to flourish

- Enhances cooperation and establishes a foundation for effective teamwork

- Improves communication between different levels in the organization

- Helps employees adapt to the changing workplace by sharing information, concerns, and possible strategies for addressing the issues

- Makes a statement about the company's values

Cost Effective

- Results in increased productivity because of the improvement in employee skills and motivation

- Reduces organizational turnover. Mentees receive individual attention and plan for their careers in the company.

- Requires minimal time commitment

Challenges of Mentoring:

- Mentee ideas could be encouraged by the mentor but not supported by the mentee's boss and consequently are not tested for their viability.

- The cost of mentoring in terms of mentor and mentee time could outweigh the benefits, particularly if the match-up of people is poor.

- Employees engaged in a mentoring relationship invest time and effort which could detract from their job responsibilities.

Benefits of Mentoring	Challenges of Mentoring

Cost Effective (cont.)

◆ Makes hiring of new employees more cost effective if young people can be mentored in intern positions and gain the appropriate training before becoming an employee

◆ Requires a low financial investment

◆ Uses talent that might not have surfaced otherwise

Leadership Development

◆ Develops future leaders, resulting in effective succession planning

◆ Creates an opportunity to promote and retain employees with leadership potential, especially women and minorities

◆ Enables future organizational leaders to develop and practice their skills

◆ Motivates mentees to work towards being effective leaders

◆ The program could be viewed as elitist and could be resented by other employees who are not included.

◆ Mentees could be recognized as having leadership potential and then not meet company expectations.

3

Benefits of Mentoring	Challenges of Mentoring

Diversity

- Advances capable individuals, particularly minorities and women

- Helps organizations to meet diversity goals

- Assists in retaining the "balance" of the organization. Mentees bring a variety of experiences and backgrounds that enrich the organization.

- Those outside the mentoring interaction could view this as exclusionary and this could result in demotivated employees.

Training

- Enables new hires to be easily assimilated into the organization

- Reduces the need for scheduled skill development training opportunities

- Provides on-the-job training

- Encourages employees to be active and lifelong learners

- Organizations could over-rely on mentors to provide quality skill development and reduce formal training opportunities that are needed.

- Those outside the mentoring interaction could view this as exclusionary, and this could result in demotivated employees.

Take a Moment

List at least three ways that mentoring would benefit your organization.

_____

_____

_____

Identify three challenges that your organization would need to confront if mentoring became a reality.

_____

_____

_____

3

In addition to the many benefits mentoring can bring to the organization, it can also greatly enhance the mentor and mentee's value as employees.

Mentor Benefits and Challenges

Benefits of Mentoring

- ◆ Develops skills in coaching, relationship-building, consulting, and teaching

- ◆ Helps to rejuvenate the long-time employee

- ◆ Assists in decision making by seeking the mentee's perspective and input

- ◆ Validates the skills and experiences gained, which gives a sense of achievement

Challenges of Mentoring

- ◆ Demands too much time and energy

- ◆ Could result in a negative experience because of a poor mentor/mentee match

- ◆ Causes resentment because employee was required to be a mentor

- ◆ Causes company expectations of mentor to be too high

Benefits of Mentoring	Challenges of Mentoring
◆ Creates a feeling of satisfaction in knowing that the mentee is learning and growing	
◆ Receives recognition in the organization for participating as a mentor	

Take a Moment

As a mentor, what are (could be) the benefits to you?

_____

_____

_____

As a mentor what are (could be) the challenges to you?

_____

_____

_____

Mentee Benefits and Challenges

Benefits of Mentoring	Challenges of Mentoring
◆ Allows the opportunity to try out ideas using the mentor as a sounding board	◆ Could result in lack of support because the mentor does not have the time for the relationship
◆ Supports career development planning	◆ Could create a negative relationship because the mentor wants to control mentee actions rather than allow the mentee to learn from his/her own actions
◆ Helps in identifying skill development needs and seeks alternatives for meeting those needs	

Benefits of Mentoring	**Challenges of Mentoring**

◆ Absorbs the new hire into the organization

◆ Suffers from lack of support by mentee's supervisor

◆ Learns about the organizational culture: its policies, procedures, systems, and relationships

3

Take a Moment

As a mentee, what are (could be) the benefits to you?

_____

_____

_____

As a mentee, what are (could be) the challenges to you?

_____

_____

_____

The benefits of mentoring, together with all the research gathered, provides good support for presenting the mentoring concept to the key company decision makers. In addition, project supporters must ensure that the goals of the mentoring initiative align closely with the organizational mission.

At this point, the mentoring project organizers might be well advised to further develop their plan before they seek official approval to go ahead. It is crucial to gain organizational commitment at the onset of the project so that resources can be made available to the project and key company employees can speak out in its support.

Step 3: Identify the Process

There are some similarities and some differences in the three different approaches to mentoring described at the beginning of this chapter. The purpose of your mentoring project will help to determine which approach to follow.

Approach	**A** Mentors and mentees are targeted	**B** Mentors and mentees are volunteers	**C** Everyone is a mentor/mentee
Purpose	Select employees for skill development.	Create opportunities for mentors to share their expertise.	Encourage informal mentoring to support the learning organization.

First Steps	• Identify mentees and their needs.
	
	• Interview mentees.
	
	• Target possible mentors.
	
	• Interview potential mentors.
	
	• Match mentee to mentor by coordinator or mentee makes mentor selection.
		• Invite employees to participate as a mentor.
		
		• Interview prospective mentors.
		
		• Create a mentor pool.
		
		• Invite employees to become a mentee and identify their areas of need.
		
		• Match mentee to mentor by coordinator or mentee makes mentor selection.
			• All employees are educated to the value of mentoring relationships and are given practical ideas for implementation including:
			  - purpose of mentoring
			  - needed skills
			  - how to select a mentor
			  - how to work to improve skills
			  - how to end a mentoring relationship
			
			• Management models mentoring at work.

A	B	C	
• Once the match is made:	• Once the match is made:	• Periodic in-service training is offered to deal with issues that emerge in the mentoring arrangements.	**Next Steps**

A

• Once the match is made:
  - Conduct an orientation.
  - Clarify expectations.
  - Come to an agreement.
  - Develop a plan.
  - Attend in-service opportunities and support meetings.
  - Evaluate relationship.

B

• Once the match is made:
  - Conduct an orientation.
  - Clarify expectations.
  - Come to an agreement.
  - Develop a plan.
  - Attend in-service opportunities and support meetings.
  - Evaluate relationship.

C

• Periodic in-service training is offered to deal with issues that emerge in the mentoring arrangements.

Next Steps

3

Take a Moment

1. Our primary purpose in developing a mentoring project is:

   ❏ To meet employee needs for specific skill development.

   ❏ To use employee expertise to support another's growth and development.

   ❏ To enhance the organizational culture.

2. Key administrators support the program.
   ❏ Yes   No

3. If response is "no," how will you gain support?

4. If response is "yes," how are they showing their support?

Step 4: Develop a Plan

The project initiators will need to develop a plan of action. The plan should include:

◆ A description of the approach that will be adopted.

◆ The date when the project will begin.

◆ How long the test period will last.

◆ Who will coordinate the effort.

◆ The resources that will be needed.

◆ How program effectiveness will be measured.

Step 5: Review the Plan with Decision Makers

In order for the mentoring project to become a reality, the initiators must return to the key decision makers for their approval and commitment of resources. They will need to show the purpose of the project and its intended outcomes in measurable terms. They will need a budget of proposed expenditures and suggested financial resources to support the effort.

In order for the mentoring program to become a reality, the initiators must return to the key decision makers for their approval and commitment of resources.

Step 6: Implement and Evaluate the Project

The following sections will give you specific ideas for recruiting and matching mentors and mentees and providing them with ongoing support.

Recruiting and Matching Participants

How to Recruit Targeted Mentees and Mentors

1. Have managers nominate individuals who they believe will benefit from a mentoring relationship. Have them state the reasons for their selection.

2. Interview prospective mentees. Ask questions such as:

◆ What do you hope to gain from a mentoring relationship?

◆ What strengths would you like your mentor to have?

◆ How would you like a mentor to assist you—as a coach to motivate, a teacher to help in skill development, a consultant to assist with problem solving, or a relationship-builder to help manage relationships?

◆ What skill areas would you like to develop?

◆ What assets do you bring to the mentoring relationship?

3. Be sure mentors and mentees understand expectations. Expectations will vary depending on the purpose of the proposed relationship and the organizational context.

3

Mentee Expectations

◆ To take responsibility for your own learning

◆ To set up appointments with your mentor and to keep those commitments

◆ To develop a personal action plan

◆ To give the time necessary for practicing skills

◆ To thank your mentor for his or her time and expertise

◆ To evaluate the success of the mentoring relationship

◆ To report to the coordinator on a regular basis

Mentor Expectations

◆ To meet regularly with your mentee

◆ To meet regularly with your mentee

◆ To enable your mentee to make his or her own decisions

◆ To provide ideas, suggestions, and strategies for your mentee to consider as options when making decisions

◆ To guide but not control

◆ To seek opportunities for your mentee to learn

◆ To be an active listener

◆ To follow through on appointments and commitments

◆ To practice confidentiality

◆ To evaluate the success of the mentoring relationship

◆ To report to the coordinator on a regular basis

How to Recruit Mentors and Mentees Who Are Not Targeted

1. Develop mentee and mentor role descriptions (see the list of Mentee and Mentor Expectations on the previous page).

2. Determine how the mentoring project will be publicized. How will you respond to the WIIFM question (What's In It For Me?) that mentees and mentors will be asking? (For help, review the Benefits of Mentoring section earlier in this chapter.)

3. Can you use some in-house vehicles for communication, such as a newsletter, e-mail, or fax system?

4. Advertise the mentoring opportunities in concrete terms stating the length of the commitment and the expectations for both partners in the relationship. Also emphasize that mentoring is a partnership through which both the mentee and mentor will learn and develop.

5. Require prospective mentees and mentors to complete an interest application form (see samples) and return to the project coordinator via fax or e-mail.

An interesting dilemma in program coordination is: *should mentoring always take place on a volunteer basis?*

Sample of a Mentee Interest Application Form

Being Mentored—Is It for Me?

Benefits:

- Develop your skills
- Discuss strategies for dealing with work-related issues
- Review career development options
- Gain support for innovative ideas
- Learn how to work more effectively with others
- Take advantage of a confidential support system
- Gain a better understanding of a company-wide perspective

I Am Interested in Finding Out More!

Name _____ Department_____

Phone _____ Fax _____E-mail _____

What is your job title? _____

How many years have you been in this position? _____

with this company? _____

What skills do you want to improve?

_____

_____

_____

What appeals to you about being a mentee?

_____

_____

_____

Thank you for your interest. You will be contacted within a week to set up a time to further discuss your application. Please fax or e-mail this form to Mary Smith at 555-2222 or MARYMENTOR@byu.com.

3

Sample of a Mentor Interest Application Form

Be a Mentor!

Benefits:

- Share your skills
  Develop skills in coaching, teaching, consulting and relationship-building
- Connect with your mentee to gain feedback on how changes are affecting others in the company
- Gain satisfaction from knowing you are "growing" the company
- Earn company recognition for taking a leadership role
- Have the partners sign a partnership agreement (see sample). This consists of a list of expectations on both sides.

I Am Interested in Finding Out More!

Name _____ Department_____

Phone _____ Fax _____E-mail _____

What is your job title? _____

How many years have you been in this position? _____

                              with this company? _____

What are your areas of skill?

_____

_____

_____

What appeals to you about being a mentor?

_____

_____

_____

Thank you for your interest. You will be contacted within a week to set up a time to further discuss your application. Please fax or e-mail this form to Mary Smith at 555-2222 or MARYMENTOR@byu.com.

How to Match Mentees and Mentors

◆ **Step 1:** Begin the matching process by developing criteria for selection. Respond to the questions "What do we need to consider in making this match?" and "What should be our priority?" If the goal of your program is skill development, your focus will be on matching skill areas. If the goal is to advance a particular group within the organization, such as women, consider matching by gender. Perhaps you want to involve people who have been with the company a certain number of years, or you want to match participants across departments. These criteria must be developed ahead of the selection process. Use the following form to help you develop selection criteria.

Begin the matching process by developing criteria for selection.

3

Criteria for Selection of Mentors

1. What are you hoping to achieve by using mentors?

   _____

   _____

2. What mentor skills are needed to accomplish that?

   _____.   _____

   _____   _____

3. What qualities/characteristics would you like your mentors to have?

   _____   _____

   _____   _____

4. How will you choose from those people who are eligible?—by skills, qualities, experience, age, position, or by recommendation?

   _____   _____

   _____   _____

5. Does the prospective mentor have the skills and qualities/characteristics that would help meet the needs of a particular mentee?

   ❏ Yes   ❏ No

Criteria for Selection of Mentees

1. What are you hoping mentees will gain from this experience?

   _____

   _____

2. What qualities and attitudes do you expect mentees to possess?

   _____

   _____

3. Has the prospective mentee identified someone he/she would like as a mentor

   ❏ Yes   ❏ No

4. Are the conditions conducive for a mentoring relationship in the department where the prospective mentee works?

   ❏ Yes   ❏ No

- **Step 2:** Review the mentee and mentor application forms.

- **Step 3:** Look for matches based on the criteria you have developed.

- **Step 4:** Have candidates review the Mentee/Mentor Expectations sheet and invite them for an interview.

- **Step 5:** Interview likely candidates for a match to verify what is on the application and to answer questions about expectations and the mentoring relationship.

- **Step 6:** Announce the match to the mentee and mentor.

- **Step 7:** Invite mentee/mentor partners to attend a meeting with other matches.

Providing Orientation and Support

After you've determined who will participate in your program, you'll need to orient them and provide ongoing support in order to make their mentoring experience a positive one.

How to Orient Your Mentees and Mentors

◆ **Step 1:** At the initial Mentee/Mentor meeting, review the expectations for the partners.

◆ **Step 2:** Have individuals who have experienced a mentoring relationship share their stories.

◆ **Step 3:** Ask for and respond to questions from the participants.

◆ **Step 4:** Give them a contact name and number if questions or concerns arise.

How to Provide Ongoing Support to Mentors and Mentees

◆ **Step 1:** The mentor and mentee should begin their work together by completing a development plan in collaboration with the mentee's supervisor. (See the following sample.) This plan should include what specific skills and career development activities the mentee will address over the next few months of the mentoring relationship.

Sample Mentee Development Plan

My Development Plan

My purpose in being a mentee is _____

_____

My goals are:

1. _____

2. _____

3. _____

My actions: what, how, and when I will achieve my goals:

Goal 1 _____

	What	How	Time Line	Completion Date
Action 1				
Action 2				
Action 3				

Goal 2 _____

	What	How	Time Line	Completion Date
Action 1				
Action 2				
Action 3				

Goal 3 _____

	What	How	Time Line	Completion Date
Action 1				
Action 2				
Action 3				

◆ **Step 2:** After one month, the mentoring partnership should be reviewed to make sure it is beginning on a strong foundation. The partnership should be evaluated again after three months and then extended, if progress is being made, to six months or a year. Mentor and mentee can sign a mentoring agreement similar to the example shown when they begin their six-month commitment.

Mentoring Agreement

We have agreed to enter into an informal, mutually beneficial partnership for a period of six months, with the option to extend to one year if we both choose.

We agree to the following:

1. To meet at least twice a month for a minimum of two hours.
2. To retain confidentiality unless my partner gives me permission to share the points of our discussion.
3. To attend bimonthly meetings with other mentors and mentees in the organization.
4. I, the Mentor, will assist my mentee to create and implement a personal development plan that will be an aid in skill improvement and career development. I will be an active listener, share my experiences and offer constructive feedback when they seem appropriate.
5. I, the Mentee, will be open to any ideas my mentor shares with me. I will use this opportunity to work on improving specific skills and examining career development options.
6. To follow through on commitments we make to each other.
7. To end our mentoring relationship if either of us so desires.

Signed _____   _____
           Mentee   Mentor

Date _____   _____

Evaluating Your Program

How to Measure the Effectiveness of Your Mentoring Project

To determine whether the mentoring project should be continued, expanded, or eliminated, you must systematically collect data, analyze it, and report your findings to all stakeholders. You will have chosen your evaluation tools when you prepared your original project plan (Step 4: Develop a Plan). Measurement should always be considered before the project begins, not as it is underway.

Your evaluation tools should measure:

◆ Whether any changes have occured (results).

◆ Whether the mentoring program system is effcient (process).

◆ Whether there were sufficient resources to develop and implement the program (resources).

You should always ask managers and key decision makers what data they would like to see collected. Their input should be used as a basis for the evaluation design. In addition to examining the overall results of the project, the mentoring participants must be surveyed to identify the successes and challenges they have experienced in their relationships.

Program Evaluation Components

As you consider the impact of the mentoring program, key questions include:

◆ Has the mentoring program caused some positive changes in the organization?

◆ Did the mentoring program operate smoothly?

◆ Do the benefits of the program outweigh the costs?

The following consideration of program, content, relationships, and results will help you answer these questions.

> Measurement should always be considered before the project begins, not as it is underway.

3

The Processes

◆ Were mentors and mentees recruited easily? Are there ways the recruitment strategies could be improved?

◆ How well do members of the organization who are not involved in the mentoring program understand what is happening?

◆ Was the communication link between participants and the coordinator appropriate for dealing with issues as they arose?

◆ What process was in place for tracking mentor and mentee follow-through on their commitment?

◆ Is the matching process efficient and effective?

The Content

◆ Did the participants understand the philosophical basis of mentoring?

◆ Did program participants find any instructional materials used to explain mentoring useful?

◆ Was the content of the training and meetings valuable?

The Relationship

Were the mentor and mentee comfortable with their partnership?

◆ Were the mentor and mentee comfortable with their partnership?

◆ Were the partners learning from each other?

◆ Has the relationship created any conflicts between the mentor and mentee? Were the conflicts managed appropriately?

◆ Did the participants understand their roles and how they were expected to relate to each other?

The Results

◆ Were enough mentors recruited to match with mentees?

◆ Did the participants attend the scheduled training sessions and meetings?

◆ How many active mentor/mentee relationships exist?

◆ How frequently do the participants meet each other?

◆ What are the costs for the program in terms of time, people, and money?

◆ How long have the mentoring relationships existed?

◆ Do the mentor/mentee matches result in the agreed-upon time commitment from the partners?

The evaluation of the mentoring program should be conducted periodically throughout the year and not left until the year is completed. By continually examining the processes, content, relationships, and results of the program, you can make ongoing changes to improve the delivery of services.

Evaluate the mentoring program periodically throughout the year; don't wait until the year is completed.

Using Program Evaluation Tools

There are a variety of methods to gather information related to program processes, content, relationships, and results. Here are some ideas:

◆ **Create a written survey.**
Develop an instrument to evaluate how effective the mentoring relationship has been. Survey recipients would include the mentor, mentee, the mentee's supervisor, and possibly employees who work with the mentee.

The survey would ask some of the questions discussed earlier that address each of the four program evaluation components.

◆ **Conduct focus groups.**
Groups of mentors and mentees can be brought together to talk about their experiences. Also, random groups of people in the company can be asked to give feedback on their perceptions of the mentoring program. A series of questions would be posed to the groups and the responses would be recorded and tabulated with other like-group responses.

◆ **Set objectives.**
You should develop program objectives before the mentoring program is implemented. These objectives state in measurable, specific terms what the program is expected to accomplish. At the end of the designated period, the current status can be measured against the objectives to see whether the objectives have been met.

◆ **Use pre- and posttests.**
An effective and simple way to determine whether any changes have occurred as a result of the mentoring program is to administer pre- and posttests. Ask mentees questions about skills and attitudes before the mentoring relationship has been established. Then ask the same questions at the end of the agreed period and compare the two sets of responses.

◆ **Conduct interviews.**
Individual mentors and mentees can be interviewed using either a formal or informal approach.

• The formal method would involve asking a set series of structured questions and recording individual answers.

• The informal approach is more conversational. The interviewer asks several open-ended questions, such as "How is the relationship working?"and allows the speaker to proceed conversationally.

The informal approach is less directed by the interviewer and can reveal information that might not surface with a more formal approach. On the other hand, when an interview is less structured, the interviewer has a greater challenge keeping the interviewee focused on relevant information. Valuable quantitative and also anecdotal data can result from both interview processes. However, this method of evaluation is very time consuming and, consequently, costly.

◆ **Examine organizational records.**
All organizations maintain records. These documents can provide valuable information in the evaluation process. Attendance records, performance appraisals, and records of productivity could all reflect the impact that the mentoring relationship has had upon the mentor and mentee.

3

◆ **Develop competency lists.**
A competency list can help you determine whether a mentee has experienced growth as a result of the mentoring relationship. The mentee, with the assistance of his or her supervisor, would list the tasks that make up the mentee's job responsibilities. The supervisor would then evaluate the mentee on whether the tasks were performed appropriately or whether they needed improvement. The mentee would ask the mentor for assistance to increase skills in the areas that are deficient. After a certain period, you can evaluate the mentee again against the competency list. Any positive changes from the previous evaluation would measure mentee growth.

> A competency list can help you determine whether a mentee has experienced growth as a result of the mentoring relationship.

◆ **Demonstrate skills.**
Another method for evaluating mentee performance is by demonstration. Once some time has elapsed in the mentoring relationship, you can measure mentee performance change in selected competencies by observing the particular skill while the mentee is on the job. Observation of the mentee at work is a valuable evaluation tool.

◆ **Conduct 360° feedback.**
Evaluation of the mentee by his or her supervisor and by peers can provide valuable information about their perceptions of the mentee's behaviors, attitudes, and skills. The feedback instrument could be administered at the beginning of the mentoring relationship and again a year later to see whether any changes have occurred. The challenge with using this evaluation strategy is finding a suitable instrument. Designing one's own feedback instrument requires specific skills and can be time consuming.

◆ **Keep a log.**
A mentee can be required to maintain a log of all mentoring activities. This log would document when meetings with the mentor occurred, what took place, the specific actions that were taken as an outcome of the interactions, and any results that could be attributed to the mentoring relationship. A mentor might also be required to keep a log or complete a monthly report form.

The selected evaluation instruments must provide information that examines the processes, the content, the relationships and the results of the mentoring program.

Selecting Evaluation Tools

The type of evaluation methods to use depend on:

◆ **The intent of the mentoring program.**
If the program is designed to build skills, demonstrations, competency lists, and pre- and posttests can all be used. If the program has been established to bring about changes in the business culture, then focus groups and surveys are more appropriate.

◆ **What information is available.**
Begin by determining what data is already being collected. For example, is an annual survey of employees already in place and can questions relating to mentoring be included? Are there organizational records that can be used as indicators of the effectiveness of the mentoring program?

◆ **To whom the program coordinator is accountable.**
If that person requires quantifiable data, then using surveys, pre- and posttests and competency lists would be the answer. On the other hand, qualitative, descriptive reports can provide more personal and in-depth information. A mix of both quantitative and qualitative data would give a more substantial view of what is happening.

◆ **Resources of time and money.**
Don't forget to consider the availability of resources as you make your decision about the type of evaluation tool to use.

Don't Forget to Celebrate!

As part of managing a mentoring program, it is crucial to celebrate every step of the way. Celebrating small accomplishments as well as major achievements is important.

3

Remembering to celebrate is an important part of managing any mentoring progam.

Cause for Celebration

◆ Mentee completes a class.

◆ A mentoring partnership is a year old (3 months old, 6 months old).

◆ Mentor agrees to work with an additional mentee.

◆ Birthdays and anniversaries.

◆ Goals are reached (50 mentors, 100 mentees, increase in productivity, employee satisfaction rating is improved).

◆ Key company decision makers become mentors.

◆ Mentor is recruited.

◆ Everything!

How to Celebrate

◆ Create a bulletin board display to spotlight a mentoring match.

◆ Send personal thank-you notes to participants.

◆ Send a letter to the participants' supervisors commending their involvement.

◆ Hold a special social event, such as a barbecue, a banquet, or a wine and cheese party. Invite key organizational leaders to attend.

◆ Write articles for the organizational newsletter.

◆ Invite the local media to hear about the positive impact mentoring has made on the organization.

◆ Distribute certificates and awards to participants.

◆ Give out tickets to special events or discount coupons to a variety of stores.

Though there are many steps involved in building a successful mentoring program, the results for mentors and mentees can truly be something to celebrate. In our next chapter, we'll look at several successful mentoring programs and consider the successes and challenges of each.

Chapter Summary

Formal programs can take a variety of approaches to mentoring. Programs can:

◆ Be highly selective when choosing their mentors and mentees.

◆ Have all volunteer mentors and mentees.

◆ Encourage everyone in the organization to become a mentor or mentee.

To develop a formal mentoring program, those organizing the program must:

◆ Determine the purpose of the program.

◆ Seek organizational commitment.

◆ Identify the mentoring process to be used.

◆ Develop a program plan.

◆ Review the plan with decision makers.

◆ Implement and evaluate the program.

Program organizers can begin implementation by recruiting participants. Be sure that mentors and mentees understand the expectations for their role and the benefits they can gain from the relationship. Develop a set of criteria to help you match the right mentor to the right mentee.

In order to determine whether the mentoring program should be continued, expanded, or eliminated, program organizers should collect data that illustrates whether participants have benefited from the experience. You can use a variety of evaluation tools, including:

◆ Written surveys

◆ Focus groups

◆ Measurement against set objectives

◆ Pre- and posttests

◆ Interviews

◆ Organizational records

◆ Competency lists

◆ Skill demonstrations

◆ 360° feedback

◆ Log entries

Throughout any mentoring program, those involved should be encouraged to celebrate their successes.

Self-Check: Chapter Three Review

Answers appear on page 127.

1. List three benefits and three challenges that can result from developing a mentoring program.

   Benefits

   a. _____

   b. _____

   c. _____

   Challenges

   a. _____

   b. _____

   c. _____

2. True or False?
   A quality mentoring program is likely to succeed with or without commitment from top management.

3. What are the six steps to follow when creating a mentoring program?

   a. _____

   b. _____

   c. _____

   d. _____

   e. _____

   f. _____

4. What are three methods you could use to evaluate your mentoring program?

   a. _____

   b. _____

   c. _____

5. Don't forget to _____ your successes!

Notes

3

Chapter*Four*

Models of Mentoring Programs

Chapter Objectives

▶ Identify a variety of successful mentoring programs.

▶ Identify those elements that have contributed to the successes and those that have resulted in challenges to the programs.

▶ Select elements that will be an aid as you develop or seek to improve your program.

Case Study

In 1995, Bruce, a trial lawyer, became involved with Partners in Education, a program that encourages businesspeople to mentor local schoolchildren. Bruce was matched with DeUndre, a fourth-grade African-American student. They started meeting for an hour each week. To win DeUndre's trust, Bruce asked him to tell stories. Bruce recorded the stories in his notebook computer and gave printouts to DeUndre. They also played games together.

As the mentoring relationship grew, DeUndre's home life was in transition. When DeUndre was in fifth grade, his mother went to prison, and DeUndre went to live with his great-aunt. At the same time, Bruce and DeUndre became involved with Big Brothers/Big Sisters and began meeting on weekends as well as during the school week. DeUndre became involved in Bruce's family activities and developed a special bond with Bruce's youngest son, Paul.

During the first semester of sixth grade, DeUndre began experiencing severe abdominal pain. Because his great-aunt had other family responsibilities, Bruce was with DeUndre when he had exploratory surgery that resulted in the removal of a cancerous tumor. After the surgery, Bruce moved into DeUndre's hospital room and remained with him for two weeks until he was discharged. Bruce also helped DeUndre through a six-month round of chemotherapy.

Bruce continues his involvment with DeUndre. "He is a wonderful person," said Bruce. "My life and that of my family has been deeply enriched by our relationship with DeUndre. I have come to the conclusion that mentors are made, not born. My mentoring abilities have been a result of those people who influenced me as I was growing up. They were willing to take risks and step outside their comfort zones to support me."

We have discussed the qualities shared by successful mentors and the steps for building a formal mentoring program. To see how the theory of mentoring is applied in different environments, we will now consider several mentoring programs that can serve as models of success. The following examples illustrate mentoring programs in a variety of settings: government, business, nonprofit organizations, education, and labor.

Model 1: FLIK Manager Trainee Program

Environment

Corporate

4

Case Study

Purpose

To develop managers and hourly employees who can take on greater responsibilities within the company. As the FLIK company continues to grow, so does its need for qualified managers.

Description

FLIK is a regional food service management company. The organization typically runs food service operations for large corporations, schools, and colleges.

This manager trainee program involves one-on-one mentoring. It is seven months long and takes the trainee through all aspects of the company from corporate history and culture to operations management. Each trainee receives personalized guidance in completing company paperwork; learning different management skills; and developing food, nutrition, sanitation, and human resource issues. An experienced Food Service Director is assigned to mentor each trainee and guides the trainee using the organization's Training Manual. Group meetings for all trainees are held every other month to assess their progress and to work on different sections of the manual.

Successes

- FLIK has graduated over 100 individuals in the eight years of the program's existence.

- Graduates have gone on to become Food Service Directors and more recently have been promoted to Group Manager level.

- Over 90 percent of the employees who have started the program have completed it.

- The Training Manual is designed to allow the trainees to work on the sections of the book that reflect what is happening currently at their unit.

Challenges

Challenge 1: Selection of Participants

Identifying and selecting the right employees for the program has been a challenge. Most of the employees who did not finish the program were not properly qualified.

Strategies

- Analyze why certain individuals did not finish the program.

- Develop an effective screening process to include pre-testing, samples of written work, and interviews with the Training Manager and the Executive Vice President.

Challenge 2: Completion of Program on Schedule

Many of the trainees were having problems completing the program in the seven months desired because of heavy workloads.

Strategy

Use the Trainee (mentee) Meetings to cover areas of the Training Manual that have been causing most of the problems for the trainees.

Model 2: FLIK School-to-Work Program

Case Study

Environment

Corporate and Education

Purpose

To graduate students from the School-to-Work Program, keep in touch with them as they go on to college, then offer them jobs upon graduation. Experts predict that in the years to come, the food service industry will suffer from a shortage of qualified employees. By developing talent early, FLIK can prepare for the future and help the community by providing jobs and education to high school students.

Description

The program is run in conjunction with local high schools that offer a culinary arts program. Student externs are paid to work in FLIK accounts, thus exposing them to operating in an upscale food service environment (vs. fast food establishments). The students spend 12 weeks working after school with a unit chef developing their skills. Students work all areas of the unit, learning about the kitchen, paperwork, conference work and, if available, executive dining. They must keep a weekly journal so their progress can be evaluated. To help evaluate the success of the program, pre- and posttests of the students are conducted.

Successes

◆ The School-to-Work Program has existed for four years.

◆ More than 30 students have graduated from the program.

Challenges

Challenge 1: No Formal Curriculum

FLIK works with a number of different agencies, and the types of programs administered by these agencies vary. No common curriculum has ever been created.

Strategies

◆ Develop an extern training manual that is flexible enough to work with any program.

◆ Develop competencies upon which the student will be evaluated in areas such as sanitation, safety, and kitchen station work; exposure to conference catering; and inventory and receiving.

◆ Have students maintain a journal that is signed weekly by both the chef and the students' instructors at school.

Challenge 2: No Employee Return

To date, FLIK has yet to have any students return to work for them after they have completed the program.

Strategies

◆ Increase contact with students who have left the program.

◆ Help students in the program find places in culinary schools. Contact with culinary schools is helping to make this happen.

FLIK International Corporation Contact:

Ron Tremper
Training and Safety Manager
FLIK International Corp.
Food Service Management
3 International Drive
Rye Brook, NY 10573
(914)-935-5300
(914)-935-5540 Fax

Model 3: Hospital Youth Mentoring Program

Environment

Corporate and Education

Case Study

Purpose

To assist at-risk youth from low-income families, matching them with mentors to help them complete high school and make the transition to postsecondary education or work.

Description

Since June 1993, the Hospital Youth Mentoring Program, administered by The Johns Hopkins Hospital and funded by The Commonwealth Fund, has supported youth mentoring projects at 15 hospitals. By involving hospitals with youth from their communities, the program not only has helped youth but also has encouraged the hospitals to take a more active role in addressing local community needs and educating their future workforce.

4

The Students

Sites have had the most success with C-average students who, though at risk of not finishing high school on time, indicate an interest in their future. These students generally are poor and have little idea how to reach their future goals but some sense that there is a future for them. They appear most able to develop a relationship with a mentor and to be motivated by a mentoring program.

Three of the programs have enrolled middle school students, two have enrolled 11th graders, and the remainder have enrolled 9th or 10th graders. At whatever age students are enrolled, the hospitals continue to provide services until they graduate from high school.

Partnership with Schools

Five of the projects build on existing relationships between the hospital and local schools; the other 10 established new relationships. Six fostered links with new or existing health academies and apprenticeship programs.

Career Orientation

Thirteen of the 15 hospitals are now in the process of making their programs more career oriented by implementing a career guide-Big Brother/Big Sister model of mentoring and expanding the school-to-career components of their programs.

The Hospitals

The 15 hospitals participating in the Hospital Youth Mentoring Program are:

◆ Albert Einstein Medical Center, Philadelphia, PA

◆ Allegheny University of the Health Sciences (formerly Hahnemann), Philadelphia, PA

◆ Barnes-Jewish Hospital, Washington University Medical Center, St. Louis, MO

◆ Beth Israel Medical Center, New York, NY

◆ Cedar-Sinai Medical Center, Los Angeles, CA

◆ Duke University Medical Center, Durham, NC

◆ Elmhurst Hospital Center, Elmhurst, NY

◆ Iowa Health System, Des Moines, IA

◆ Maine Medical Center, Portland, ME

◆ MetroHealth System, Cleveland, OH

◆ University of Michigan Medical Center, Ann Arbor, MI

◆ Mt. Sinai Medical Center, New York, NY

◆ University of Rochester/Strong Memorial Hospital, Rochester, NY

◆ Vanderbilt University Medical Center, Nashville, TN

◆ Washington Hospital Center, Washington, DC

Successes

- ◆ Volunteerism has increased at the medical centers, with 76 percent of the mentors stating they would continue to be a mentor in the program.

- ◆ The program forges stronger connections between the hospitals and the communities.

- ◆ Students who have participated in the mentoring program return to the hospital to work once they have graduated from high school.

- ◆ Many of the at-risk students are graduating from high school and going on to college.

- ◆ Each hospital has been able to learn from the other hospitals' experiences. The program coordinators at each of the hospitals meet semiannually. Moving from a traditionally competitive relationship, the hospitals have become collaborators.

- ◆ The maturity level of student participants has changed noticeably. They set career and skill development goals for themselves and view their futures as exciting.

- ◆ Each hospital had strong CEO support for the project. This crucial commitment contributed greatly to the programs' successes.

Challenges

Challenge 1: Change in the Health-Care Industry

The health-care industry has changed substantially in recent years. Budget cuts and reorganization have resulting in downsizing, job loss, and service reduction.

4

Strategies

◆ None of the 15 hospitals involved has dropped its mentoring program despite the pressures of tightening purse strings.

◆ CEO commitment from each program's beginning has ensured its survival.

Challenge 2: Cost

Providing students with paid internships meant financial difficulties for some of the programs.

Strategies

◆ The member hospitals looked for alternative funding sources.

◆ Johns Hopkins Hospital, as the administrator for the Hospital Youth Mentoring Program, assisted the hospitals in approaching foundations, writing grants, and using other fund-development strategies.

Challenge 3: Training

Quality training of mentors and mentees is crucial for a successful program.

Strategies

◆ Provide appropriate education for mentors and mentees so that they understand their roles and responsibilities and how to make the relationship rewarding for both partners.

◆ Ensure during the recruitment process that mentors are participating for the "right" reason. These students need help in developing their skills. They can make their own decisions about how they live their lives.

◆ Mentors meet monthly at each hospital to share their experiences and to take advantage of opportunities for increasing their skills.

Hospital Youth Mentoring Program Contact:
Deborah Knight-Kerr
Director of Community and Education Projects
The Johns Hopkins Hospital
600 N. Wolf St.
Houck 316
Baltimore, MD 21287-1454

Model 4: Cyanamid Agricultural Products Mentoring Program

Case Study

Environment

Corporate

Purpose

4

To help new sales employees make the transition from the training environment to their own sales territory.

Description

The Cyanamid Agricultural Products Group is a subsidiary of American Home Products Corporation and is the eighth largest crop protection chemical company in the world. Their mentoring program, which began in 1994, matches Master Sales Representatives with newly hired sales personnel who are in training. Within the first few days of training, the new hire resumes are sent out to the Master Sales Representatives who have agreed to be mentors. The coordinator makes the matches based on mentor input, common interests, or backgrounds, but not on geography. The mentors are then assigned to their trainees.

Within the first two months, trainees go on the road with their mentors so that they can observe the Master Sales Representatives at work. The mentors give verbal feedback on the trainees, and the trainees complete a report of what they learned.

After about four months, the trainees ride with their mentors again but are given specific tasks to do, such as making a presentation or developing customer approach strategies. The mentors then observe the trainees and give feedback on what went well and what skills should be developed.

Successes

◆ Trainees learn the history and culture of the company by working with their mentors.

◆ Trainees can "hot practice." They are given an opportunity to show how well they can perform in an environment similar to the one they will be working in when they have their own territory.

◆ Trainees are exposed to a different geographical area.

◆ Master Sales Representatives gain satisfaction from using their skills to help the newer sales employees.

◆ Master Sales Representatives can fulfill their roles as mentors as part of the personal performance expectations that they set together with their supervisors.

Challenges

Challenge 1: Geography
The trainees are all together at one location for an average of six months. Their mentors can be located anywhere in the country. The logistics of combining schedules and making the necessary travel arrangements are time consuming.

Strategies
◆ Have one person coordinate all the schedules.

◆ Have the trainees contact their mentors to arrange agreeable times for the field trips.

Challenge 2: Communication
Mentor and mentee usually meet face-to-face only twice.
Ongoing communication between the mentor and trainee takes
place by phone or e-mail, so the relationships are usually of a
professional nature only.

Strategies
◆ Encourage personal relationships with other sales staff at the
training center.

◆ Encourage regular and frequent contact between the mentor
and mentee.

Challenge 3: Busy Schedules
Master Sales Representatives are very busy people. Becoming a
mentor adds more responsibilities to their job.

Strategies
◆ Give company-wide recognition to the Master Sales
Representatives for their mentoring efforts.

◆ Have the trainees write to their mentors stating how they
have specifically helped them. Send a copy of the letter to
the Master Sales Representatives' supervisors.

Challenge 4: Giving Negative Feedback
Master Sales Representatives have difficulty giving negative
feedback to their trainees.

Strategies
◆ Give the Master Sales Representatives training on how to
give constructive feedback.

◆ Discourage mentors from sharing their concerns with the
coordinator and encourage them to give direct feedback to
their trainees.

◆ Seek opportunities to bring the mentors and trainees in
more contact, so that a greater degree of trust can develop.

4

Challenge 5: Lack of Ongoing Mentoring

The sales trainees have skills development and behavioral concerns that surface outside of the time that contact is made with their mentors.

Strategy

Use a just-in-time mentoring approach. As a concern arises, match the trainee's need with a salesperson who has the skill to help in that particular area.

American Cyanamid Contact:

William Clark
Director Sales Development
American Cyanamid
One Campus Dr.
Parsippany, NJ 07054

Case Study

Model 5: Iowa Volunteer Mentor Program

Environment

Government

Purpose

To mobilize volunteer mentors who guide and support PROMISE JOBS participants to become self-reliant through individual growth, job retention, and economic stability. Many of these individuals are transitioning off welfare.

Description

Volunteers are trained through the Iowa Volunteer Mentor Program to assist Family Investment Program/PROMISE JOBS participants in their transition towards self-sufficiency. This initiative is part of an enormous effort in Iowa to move people off welfare and into jobs through a variety of training and support programs.

The mentor program recruits former Family Investment Program participants who have successfully demonstrated self-sufficiency for at least one year and other individuals who are interested in helping this population. Mentors are matched to mentees and then receive extensive training on the mentoring process, communication, decision making, confidentiality, sensitivity, reporting, evaluation, and accessing community resources.

Successes

◆ The program operates in five cities and will expand in up to 10 cities by July 1999.

◆ In state fiscal year 1997, 71 mentoring matches were made.

◆ Mentors have been recruited through churches, synagogues, civic organizations, businesses, and women's organizations, in addition to successful graduates from the program.

◆ A number of mentors have several years with the mentoring program. They have returned to work with new mentees once their previous commitment is completed.

Challenges

Challenge 1: Required Reports

Mentors and mentees are required to complete a report of activities on a monthly basis; however, this is not happening consistently.

Strategies

◆ Provide a variety of options for reporting. A written report is one option. Reporting via the Internet and voice messaging are two other options.

◆ Clearly explain at the match meeting why reporting is necessary and that all the information is confidential.

Challenge 2: Poor Follow-Through by the Mentoring Partners

Once a match is made, the mentor and mentee should meet regularly to determine how the mentee can best meet his or her goals. This does not always happen.

Strategies

◆ At the match meeting, the program coordinator should give the mentor and mentee time to get to know each and to begin to build the trust necessary for an effective relationship.

◆ Encourage the mentor and mentee to meet soon after the match meeting in order to solidify the relationship and to keep motivation for making positive changes at a high level. Follow up with them within two weeks to confirm that a first meeting was scheduled. The longer the gap in communication, the more difficult it is for the partners to make contact.

◆ The coordinator must keep in regular touch with the mentoring partners. A telephone call, a note, or a newsletter are all good ways to remind the partners to follow-through on their commitments.

Challenge 3: Recruiting Mentees

The system for recruiting PROMISE JOBS participants into the mentoring program was not always effective.

Strategies

◆ Collaborate with the PROMISE JOBS staff so that when clients first access the program, they hear about the benefits of having a mentor.

◆ Attend the orientation for the PROMISE JOBS participants.

◆ Talk to individual PROMISE JOBS staff to ensure they are aware of the mentoring program and the benefits that clients can gain from taking advantage of this opportunity for support.

◆ Encourage the counselors who work with PROMISE JOBS clients to use a check list that includes the mentoring coordinator's telephone number and materials about the program. The counselors would check off those items on the list when the information has been passed on to each client.

◆ Obtain a list of PROMISE JOBS clients as they enter the program and follow up with a phone call to inform clients of the benefits to be gained from a mentoring relationship. There is a confidentiality issue here that is still being addressed.

Challenge 4: Matching Partners

Matching the appropriate mentors to mentees is always a challenge.

Strategies

◆ Expect the unexpected! Sometimes the best matches are those that were questionable at the outset. Don't think that professional men and women are unable to relate to former welfare recipients. Often, they are excellent mentors because they frequently have a caring, nonjudgmental attitude and lots of patience.

◆ As the mentees who enter the program have increasingly greater obstacles that challenge them, organizing a team approach to mentoring could be the answer. Mentees could be placed with several mentors who could provide assistance in a variety of capacities. Conversely, two mentees with similar needs could be assigned to one mentor. The mentees not only receive support from their mentor but also from their peer.

4

Iowa Volunteer Mentor Program Contact:
Jane E. Schockemoehl
State Coordinator
Volunteer Mentor Program
Workforce Development Administration Center
150 Des Moines Street
Des Moines, IA 50309
(515) 281-9052
(515) 281-9096 Fax

Case Study

Model 6: Choices—Peer Education Program

Environment

Education and Community

Purpose

To have secondary school students educate older elementary students about the dangers of substance abuse.

Objective

◆ To assist older elementary students to learn more about substance abuse use.

◆ To allow mentors to examine their own values and beliefs regarding substance use.

◆ To enhance the younger students' abilities to say "no" to tobacco, drugs, and alcohol and to encourage youth to choose drug-free activities over use of substances.

◆ To provide information about community resources related to substance use.

Description

Secondary students from five schools in Grey and Bruce Counties, Ontario, Canada, were selected to provide training to older elementary students from nine area feeder schools. Small discussion groups facilitated by a pair of peer educators met to define substance abuse. Participants also examined their own values and beliefs and shared positive alternatives to the use of drugs, alcohol, and tobacco. Class participation and group interaction were strongly encouraged through the use of role-play and activity-based exercises. The in-class sessions took place over a three-week period.

Successes

◆ **Peers mentoring peers**
The elementary school children have been very receptive to the presentations by the secondary students. Comments include "I am glad that it is teenagers speaking to us instead of adults who don't really know what we go through," and "I had fun and the peer presenters are good teachers."

◆ **Participatory activities**
The hands-on activities were a huge success with the participants. They particularly enjoyed learning through role-play.

◆ **Changes in Perception**
Elementary students involved in the "Choices" program reported having a better understanding of how to make responsible choices and learning the skills to say "no" to using tobacco, drugs, and alcohol.

Challenges

Challenge 1: Gaining Administrative Support
Most school administrators gave verbal support, but action did not always follow. For example, not all written communications funneled through the participating schools were delivered to the Peer Educators and teacher contacts.

Strategies
◆ Create a process for selecting administrators who would be willing to invest their time and energy into the Peer Education Program.

◆ Meet with the administrators rather than solicit their assistance by letter. Personal contact makes a greater impact than any written communication. Administrators are overwhelmed with paperwork!

Challenge 2: Geography

The large geographic area covered by the participating schools made it difficult to keep everyone informed and supportive of each other.

Strategies

◆ Target participants in the same geographic areas as cluster groups to participate and support each other.

◆ Create an electronic system of communication that would keep everyone in touch and alleviate the sense of isolation.

Challenge 3: Selection

Both peer helpers and teacher contacts need to be carefully selected so that there is real commitment to the initiative.

Strategies

◆ Create a much more thorough interview process for peer helpers that would include a written component that would require them to give more thought to what they would be doing.

◆ Allow the teacher contacts the time to decide whether they would like to volunteer in that capacity, rather than to be told to participate at the last moment.

Challenge 4: Training

Educators at the participating schools did not have a clear understanding of the Peer Education Program goals.

Strategy

Provide in-service training for all teachers and administrators on the purpose, benefits, processes, and intended outcomes of the Peer Education Program.

Challenge 5: Ownership

The coordination of the Peer Education program occurred through the Community Network Support Team, which is part of the Grey-Bruce Community Health Corporation. The schools involved in the project did not take full ownership of the project.

Strategy

Recruit key members representing each of the schools in the early stages of the program's development, so that they have an investment in the success of the venture.

4

Choices Peer Education Program Contact:

Mary Low, Community Development Worker
Community Network Support Team
Grey-Bruce Addiction Prevention Committee
1139 2nd Ave. East
Owen Sound, Ontario, Canada
(519)371-4551
(519)371-6138 Fax

Model 7: The Iowa Union-Based School-to-Work Mentoring Project

Environment

Case Study

Labor and Education

Purpose

To develop meaningful relationships between secondary students and workers. These relationships are based on communication about the wide variety of basic, technical, interpersonal, and critical-thinking skills that make up an organized set of workplace competencies. The project gives organized working people an avenue through which to share their stories with students.

Description

Iowa has a network of central labor councils, and it is within this structure that the program was organized. Each central labor council designated a local coordinator. Mentees (the students) are recruited through the local schools. Mentors attend a four-hour training session and agree to meet at least four times a semester with the student. Mentors show examples of job performance and the skills needed to be an excellent employee, and provide an entrance into the workplace culture. Mentors also spend time with their mentees in school to learn about the students' school experiences.

Successes

◆ Federal funding has been available to reimburse Local Coordinators for lost time on the job. However, many local unions and employers have shown their support of this School-to-Work project by providing reimbursement themselves.

◆ The program developed a four-hour training that prepared mentors for their roles with students. It covered the background and philosophy of labor and workforce development issues, workforce competencies, and the mentoring experience and provided an interactive guided self-assessment of workplace competencies. This training can be replicated by other union-based efforts.

◆ A manual, *Creating a Union-Based School-to-Work Mentoring Program,* was developed that gives a step-by-step description of how the project was coordinated and some of the issues that were addressed along the way.

◆ The partnerships between the schools, sponsoring labor organizations, and mentors is a successful outcome of the project. This collaborative approach is the basis of School-to-Work initiatives and is essential for bringing about systemic changes in education.

◆ Participants from the schools, both adults and students, have gained a better understanding of the labor movement, the wide range of work opportunities available, and the skills necessary to succeed as employees in the challenging work environments visited.

Challenges

Challenge 1: Making Contacts in the Schools
Program coordinators do not always know whom to contact in the schools.

Strategies
◆ Make public presentations and invite interested people to come forward.

◆ Make contacts through any personal connections.

◆ Contact the teachers who are working with job skills classes. These teachers are the greatest supporters of the program in education because they see the direct benefit to the students who are mentored.

◆ Contact with upper-level administrative personnel often takes much longer to achieve the desired result—a commitment for students to participate.

Challenge 2: Determining Which Schools to Contact
The culture in some schools is more conducive to non-traditional learning opportunities.

Strategies
◆ Approach alternative schools first. These schools allow for much more flexibility than conventional schools in terms of class content, scheduling, and teaching methods. Alternative high school students experience success as mentees because they tend to thrive in one-to-one relationships.

◆ Approach schools that have a reputation for being innovative.

4

Challenge 3: Mentoring in a Hazardous Environment

Some work environments generate questions about student safety, for example, on construction sites or around mechanical equipment.

Strategies

◆ Be knowledgeable about the age limits at the different sites. Some hazardous environments might require students to be at least 18.

◆ Take the students to the work site after hours when production has ceased for the day.

◆ Create a work sample simulation that can be organized at an apprentice training facility.

Challenge 4: Scheduling Training

Organizing training sessions was difficult because of everyone's busy and different schedules.

Strategies

◆ Offer a limited number of training times with the expectation that the mentors will attend.

◆ Link training to other already scheduled meetings.

◆ Let mentors in their own areas determine the best training times.

◆ Hold a single training event for all mentors and interested individuals during the summer. Include speakers, round table discussions and workshops that would not be available during the usual training session. Also, organize the training in a central location and at a place where the mentors and their families can enjoy some family activities. Family members are able to see what the mentoring activity involves and, consequently, lend their support to the effort.

Challenge 5: Not Enough Mentors

Requests from students seeking a mentor can outnumber the mentors who are available.

Strategy

◆ Place more than one student with a mentor. The students learn not only from the mentors but also from their peers.

◆ Consider a team approach to mentoring. A team of mentors would work with a group of students. Not only would the students benefit from a one-on-one experience, which would be arranged, but also from interaction with several mentors with different viewpoints and experiences.

Iowa Union-Based School-to-Work Mentoring Project
Jan Smith
South Central Iowa Federation of Labor, AFL-CIO
2000 Walker, Suite B
Des Moines, IA 50317
(515)-265-1042
(515)-263-2670 Fax

4

Model 8: Big Brothers/Big Sisters of Greater Des Moines, Iowa

Environment

Nonprofit

Case Study

Purpose

Big Brother/Big Sisters of America is committed to positive youth development. This is achieved by providing and supporting:

◆ Nurturing relationships between youth and adults.

◆ Guidance in the exploration of life's opportunities.

Description

Big Brother/Big Sisters pairs adults and couples with children who are lacking adequate adult influence in their lives. The relationships that develop between the adults and the children help the children grow into responsible, mature adults and provide support for them as they cope with their often difficult life situations.

Little Brothers and Little Sisters are matched between the ages of 5 and 14 and must have parent/guardian consent to enter the program. Staff members carefully assess, orient, and match volunteers with the children. Areas of common interest, expectations, age preferences, time commitment, and geographic proximity are factors that are considered. Volunteers agree to commit to their Little Brother or Little Sister for one year.

Successes

◆ Volunteers are asked to commit to one year with a child. The average mentoring relationship lasts for two and a half years.

◆ The majority of matches do work. This can be attributed to the amount of time spent in assessing both the mentee and prospective mentor. A potential Big Brother, Big Sister, or Married Couple have to complete a lengthy application form, an enforcement record check, a driving record check, and two interviews, including a home visit, before being considered for a match.

◆ There are 149 children on the waiting list for a mentor or mentor couple. This indicates the success of the program but also illustrates a challenge—how to recruit sufficient mentors to meet the needs of the children.

Challenges

Challenge 1: Recruitment
Organizers have difficulty recruiting sufficient mentors, especially males, to meet the demand.

Strategies
◆ Target married couples to mentor a child. Demographics for the Des Moines area indicate increasingly larger numbers of married couples opting not to have children or postponing having children until a later date. These young married couples should be an excellent resource pool. A Recruitment

Challenge in 1997 focused on married couples and males and netted 20 new volunteers. Current Big Brothers/Big Sisters and Couple Match volunteers received incentives to recruit new volunteers to the program.

◆ Pictures on brochures and other publicity pieces show male Big Brothers because that is where the greatest need exists. Many client families that are headed by a single female recognize the advantages of the regular presence of a Big Brother and the boys, in particular, greatly benefit from a role model.

◆ Review the application process. Is it possible to gather all the necessary information by using a shortened application form and more in-depth interviews? Currently, it takes about two hours to complete the application form. Responding to all the questions does indicate a real interest, but does it also "turn off" some excellent prospects?

Challenge 2: Communication
Once the mentor or mentor couple is matched with a mentee, the participants take the responsibility for the partnership. It takes great effort for the partners and the agency to keep in touch.

Strategies
◆ Staff should contact the mentoring partners on a monthly basis by phone.

◆ The mentor and mentee family should also talk to staff regularly to report how the partnership is progressing and any difficulties that have been encountered. This expectation is explained to the mentor prior to the signing of a mentoring agreement.

◆ Meetings for mentors to network with other mentors and for educational offerings that will help them in their partnership with "Littles" should also assist with communication.

◆ Use e-mail to keep in touch.

4

Challenge 3: Funding

Big Brothers/Big Sisters is a nonprofit agency that depends on United Way funds and its own fundraising efforts.

Strategies

◆ Pursue all the traditional funding activities, such as fundraising events, corporate sponsors, fund drives, and grant writing.

◆ Charge a user fee for the matching service.

◆ Gain recognition in the community as the experts on mentoring to avoid duplicate efforts by other organizations.

◆ Expand agency offerings to include a matching service to assist other organizations setting up mentoring partnerships.

Big Brothers/Big Sisters Contact:

Althea Holcomb, Executive Director
Big Brothers/Big Sisters of Greater Des Moines
333 S.W. 9th Street
Des Moines, IA 50309
(515)-288-9025
(515)-288-6191 Fax

You have read about a wide range of mentoring programs in a variety of settings. There are many more excellent mentoring activities existing in the corporate, nonprofit, labor, education, and government environments. Unfortunately, space limits the inclusion of additional models.

Self-Check: Chapter Four Review

1. List three ideas that you gained from these examples of successful mentoring programs that you can use in your own program.

   a. _____

   b. _____

   c. _____

2. What steps will you take to integrate these ideas into your mentoring strategies?

   a. _____

   b. _____

   c. _____

3. List the contact persons and the companies that you believe can help with your mentoring activities.

   _____

   _____

   _____

4

Chapter *Five*

Troubleshooting Guide

Chapter Objectives

▶   Identify possible program coordination problems.

▶   View challenges from the mentee and mentor perspectives.

▶   Identify successful strategies to address the issues.

Despite careful planning and the best of intentions, mentoring relationships can encounter problems. Some problems are minor and easily addressed; others are major and threaten the entire relationship.

The following challenges can impact a mentoring program and can influence the interaction between the mentor and mentee. The suggestions are ideas about how these challenges might be addressed.

Program Challenges

Program Challenge 1

Few members of the organization express enthusiasm for mentoring.

Suggestions

Make sure you have the commitment and endorsement of top management.

◆   Make sure you have the commitment and endorsement of top management. They must help to create an organization where mentoring is an integral part of the culture. Remember that a personal presentation will make a greater impression than any written communication.

- Publicize the benefits of mentoring in company newsletters, e-mail messages, and on bulletin boards. Answer the question WIIFM (What's In It For Me?).

- Recruit a highly visible upper-level manager as a mentor. This will show company commitment to the initiative.

- Recruit "movers and shakers" in the organization to participate. Their involvement will give credibility to the program and ensure that mentoring activities do occur.

- Gather participant testimonials and share them company-wide.

Program Challenge 2

The mentoring program has the perception of being for "winners" or "losers."

Suggestions

5

- Rather than making mentoring opportunities available only to specific groups or to those identified as having management potential, open up the chance to participate across the company.

- When selecting participants, emphasize commitment to the process rather than any other discriminating characteristic.

Program Challenge 3

Organizers have difficulty finding enough mentors to meet mentee requests.

Suggestions

- Make being a mentor a privilege by setting high expectations. Don't lower standards for selection in order to recruit more mentors to the program.

- Publicize mentoring success stories in terms of the individual growth of both mentors and mentees. Everyone wants to be part of a winning program!

Make being a mentor a privilege by setting high expectations.

♦ At a company function, recognize those people who have participated in the mentoring program.

♦ Use current mentors to recruit new mentors.

♦ Recruit the CEO as a mentor.

Program Challenge 4

The mentor/mentee partnership is not very active.

Suggestions

♦ Ensure up front that the mentee and mentor are clear on program expectations including frequency and duration of meetings, and roles and responsibilities.

From the beginning, ensure that mentees and mentors understand program expectations.

♦ Analyze why the partnership doesn't seem to be working. Does the mentee fail to contact the mentor for a particular reason? Has the mentor not been able to meet with the mentee because of lack of time or some other reason? Has a particular incident occurred that has changed the relationship?

♦ Facilitate a session for the mentor and mentee to discuss what is happening. Assist them in either renewing their commitment to each other or agreeing to part because the relationship doesn't seem to be meeting their needs.

♦ Organize periodic meetings for all the mentors and mentees in the program. They can take time to share their successes and their concerns and seek solutions for improving their partnerships. Members of the group support each other and this helps to motivate everyone to continue.

Program Challenge 5

The mentor/mentee match doesn't seem to work.

Suggestions

♦ If the suggestions for addressing Challenge 4 don't positively impact the mentoring relationship, then it could be time to end the partnership. This should be accomplished by following the guidelines established at the beginning of the mentoring arrangement. Don't forget to conduct a personal exit interview with both the mentor and mentee. What you discover from these conversations might contribute to improvements in your program.

◆ On the other hand, it might be possible to adhere to the mentoring agreement even though it is not totally satisfactory. If there are still benefits gained by each of the partners, it might be worthwhile to continue. This approach emphasizes the value of commitment to the relationship and can teach both partners how to gain some positive outcomes even when circumstances are not ideal.

◆ It is possible that another mentor could be matched with the mentee, while retaining the original mentor in a minimal capacity.

Program Challenge 6

The major supporter/coordinator for mentoring moves away and the program dies.

5

Suggestions

◆ Build a broad base of support for the mentoring initiative from the start. Create a mentoring committee that is composed of a cross section of organizational members, including top management and entry-level workers.

Build a broad base of support for the mentoring initiative from the start.

◆ Recruit organizational "movers and shakers" to the program.

◆ From the beginning of the program, consider succession planning. Perhaps there is an individual who could act as a deputy to the major supporter/coordinator and so take over when the change in leadership occurs.

◆ Make the program as self-sufficient as possible. If the mentors and mentees are responsible for their own relationships, chances are that the arrangement will continue whether or not there is a change in leadership.

♦ To ensure the continuation and longevity of the program, establish the mentoring relationships as a voluntary arrangement. Imposing a relationship on either a mentor or mentee will likely lead to resentment and an unproductive interaction.

Challenges from the Mentee Perspective

Mentee Challenge 1

I am uncomfortable calling my mentor because she or he is in the upper echelon of the company.

Suggestions

♦ Be clear at the beginning of the relationship how contact will be made.

♦ The mentee should not feel so intimidated by the mentor's position that approaching the mentor for assistance is difficult. Mentor orientation should address this issue.

> The mentor must state any limits on mentee contact when the agreement is first made.

♦ The mentor must state any limits on mentee contact when the agreement is first made. This might be at particular times of the day or on special occasions. However, with the use of voice mail and e-mail, the mentor can respond when it suits her or his schedule.

♦ Arrange to meet in neutral locations where the equality of the partnership can be emphasized.

Mentee Challenge 2

I am not learning very much from my mentor anymore.

Suggestions

♦ It could be time to find a new mentor. As the mentee learns and improves skills, his or her needs change. The mentor might not be able to continue to meet those mentee needs.

♦ When a mentee or mentor experiences a change in job, the interests of the partners may no longer be compatible. Again, finding a new mentor or recruiting an additional mentor can result in a more mutually satisfying relationship.

◆ Mentees should be reminded that a mentor is not responsible for all mentee learning. The mentee must use other avenues of education to supplement the growth that results from the mentoring relationship. Examples of other resources can be interacting with other people, attending classes, reading books, and researching via the Internet.

Mentee Challenge 3

My mentor tells me what to do whenever I bring up a situation that is confronting me.

Suggestions

◆ The program coordinator should ensure during training that mentors understand their role as supporter, not dictator.

◆ Mentees should impress upon their mentors that they are very appreciative of their suggestions. However, decisions about what actions to take rest squarely on the shoulders of the mentees.

5

◆ Some mentees may not be assertive. Part of mentee development should include training in assertiveness skills.

> Part of mentee development should include training in assertiveness skills.

◆ Mentees should approach their mentors with whatever challenging situation is confronting them and a list of possible solutions they have developed and ask for the mentors' opinion of the options. Some mentees might need considerable assistance in developing ideas to address problems. The emphasis should be on a proactive approach to problem solving rather than one that is reactive.

Mentee Challenge 4

I get fired up about my job after I have met with my mentor, but when I return to my work environment, I lose my enthusiasm.

Suggestions

◆ Mentees can find it very difficult to implement new strategies if their work environment is not conducive to innovation. Confirm at the beginning of the mentoring relationship that the mentee's supervisor supports the arrangement and will be open to mentee growth. Gaining input from the supervisor as the mentoring agreement is negotiated is advisable.

◆ Securing high-level commitment to mentoring should create a work culture where individuals feel encouraged to attempt new ways for improving their productivity and services to customers.

◆ Providing ongoing updates and education on mentoring program activities will enable supervisors to be more accepting of changes in mentee behavior. The confidential nature of the mentor-mentee relationship, of course, must be safeguarded.

Mentee Challenge 5

Other people in my department resent my partnership with my mentor.

Suggestions

◆ Mentees should share with their peers the benefits of having a mentor and that the relationship is a mutually beneficial arrangement.

◆ Mentees should encourage their colleagues to participate in mentoring and seek mentors themselves or enter a mentoring program.

Challenges from the Mentor Perspective

Mentor Challenge 1

My mentee never seems to take my advice, even though I have a lot more experience and education.

Suggestions

◆ One of the most important skills for a mentor to develop is listening. The mentor must have faith that the mentee can arrive at a solution to the problem presented. The mentee simply needs to test out theories by using the mentor as a sounding board. Listening is the key. By jumping in with a solution immediately, the mentor restricts the mentee's growth in problem-solving skills.

◆ A mentor can certainly have great ideas for addressing a problem, but learning takes place by allowing the mentee to practice possible strategies and to make mistakes.

◆ Let the mentee know that you are willing to share your expertise and experience to generate ideas but that the choice of which option is chosen is in the hands of the mentee.

◆ Be open to the reality of the mentoring experience. It is an equal-partner arrangement where both individuals expect to learn and grow.

◆ The mentor should ask the mentee if there is something in the approach used that is a barrier to the mentee asking for input. Perhaps the mentor and mentee have different learning styles, which can create some communication challenges. For example, the mentor may be very concerned about facts and figures, whereas the mentee prefers to discuss concepts, theories, and ideas.

Mentor Challenge 2

I spend many hours with my mentee over a month's time, but I don't seem to be growing much from the relationship.

Suggestions

◆ Reexamine the expectations laid out in the mentoring agreement. Ask questions such as, "Were my expectations realistic?" and "What is missing from the relationship?" Mentoring must be beneficial to both partners to be successful. The mentor should first express the concern with the mentee. If the mentoring agreement needs to be renegotiated, the program coordinator should be invited to give input.

> To succeed, mentoring must be beneficial to both partners.

◆ A mentor should regard the mentoring arrangement as an opportunity to refine skills, such as relationship building and problem solving.

119

◆ Asking for ideas and thoughts on issues that the mentor is addressing can result in a better understanding of another employee's perspective, and the ideas could be an aid in the problem-solving process.

Mentor Challenge 3

Sometimes I feel as though my mentee's supervisor and I are working at cross purposes.

Suggestions

◆ Obtain supervisor agreement when the mentee's plan of action is developed.

◆ Involve the mentee's supervisor from the beginning of the mentoring arrangement. The mentor and supervisor should keep in close contact so that the greatest benefit can be gained by the mentee. New skills, ideas, and strategies need to be tested by the mentee. Supervisor approval is essential for this to happen.

> **The mentor and supervisor should keep in close contact so that the most benefit can be gained by the mentee.**

Mentor Challenge 4

I don't know when I should speak out and when I should keep quiet.

Suggestions

◆ Being a mentor is somewhat of a balancing act. A mentor should know the appropriate time to make strong recommendations to the mentee and when to let the mentee follow his or her own direction. Obviously, when health and safety are at issue, the mentor must speak up. Also, mentors should stress that mistakes are acceptable as long as learning is the result and a successful and productive employee is the ultimate outcome.

◆ Never force the mentoring relationship. Mentors should take a cautious approach in the initial stages until the mentee's needs, personality, and behaviors become apparent. A mentor should be perceived as supportive by the mentee, not too inquisitive on the one hand or indifferent on the other.

Mentor Challenge 5

I'm not entirely comfortable mentoring someone of the opposite sex.

Suggestions

◆ Cross-gender mentoring can provide its own challenges. The mentor should examine the reason for the discomfort. Is it because others in the organization are exerting pressure? Is it because of fear generated by sexual harassment legislation? Is it because the male and female history and roles in the organization are so different that a common ground is hard to find?

◆ Cross-gender relationships are more noticeable in an organization. Actions that would be accepted as normal for a same-sex mentoring partnership can be misconstrued. In order to make a cross-gender relationship function effectively, the partners should keep some distance. This tempers the approach that would be encouraged in same-sex mentoring.

◆ Mentor and mentee should focus on the desired outcomes for their relationship and not get sidetracked by outside pressures or a growth of inappropriate intimacy.

◆ Discussion of the cross-gender issue between mentor, mentee, and program coordinator is essential should discomfort continue so that the partners can deal with the problem as a team.

◆ Suggest to the program coordinator that a high-level manager be invited to participate in a cross-gender mentoring relationship with a mentee. The manager can be a role model and show how effective mentoring can take place. Acceptance of cross-gender mentoring depends so much on how the organizational culture values and supports it.

◆ If the mentor's uneasiness continues, it would be advisable for the mentor to leave the relationship and seek a same-sex mentoring arrangement.

5

Conclusion

We have considered the qualities and roles of successful mentors and the steps necessary to develop and maintain a formal mentoring program. Although mentoring has many challenges, the rewards it can bring to your organization, your community, and the lives of your participants are substantial.

Challenge Assessment

1. I am:
   - ❑ A program coordinator
   - ❑ A mentor
   - ❑ A mentee

2. I face the following mentoring challenges:

   a. _____

   b. _____

   c. _____

   d. _____

3. Where can you obtain some ideas to help you meet those challenges?

   a. This Troubleshooting Guide _____

   b. _____

   c. _____

   d. _____

Self-Check: Chapter Five Review

Answers appear on page 128.

1. Give three suggestions for recruiting mentors to the program.

   a. _____

   b. _____

   c. _____

2. Mentors are sometimes uncomfortable with mentoring someone of the opposite sex. Which of the following is *not* a way to deal with such a situation?

   a. If a mentor is uncomfortable with cross-gender mentoring, the mentor, mentee, and program coordinator should discuss the situation.

   b. The mentor should simply try to ignore the discomfort and hope it will go away.

   c. If the mentor's discomfort continues, the mentor should leave the relationship and seek a same-sex mentoring arrangement.

3. True or False?
   A mentor and mentee should stay in a mentoring relationship even if the mentee has "outgrown" the mentor's skills?

4. Why should a mentor *not* tell a mentee what to do, even though the mentor has more knowledge and skills?

   _____

   _____

4. What are your options? What are the pros and cons of each option?

	Options	Pros	Cons
Challenge #1			
Challenge #2			

5. My selected option for dealing with Challenge 1:

_____

_____

6. My selected option for dealing with Challenge 2:

_____

_____

5

Answers to Chapter Reviews

Chapter One (page 22)

1. a. It is based on trust.
   b. It is mutually beneficial.
   c. It is power-free.

2. a. Coach
   b. Consultant
   c. Teacher
   d. Relationship-builder

3. a. Open minded
   b. Empathetic
   c. Lifelong learner
   d. Good communicator
   e. Talented
   f. Responsible
   g. System smart

4. A formal program is structured.
   Informal mentoring just evolves.

Chapter Two (page 48)

1. True—Sometimes you will act as a motivator (coach), or you will instruct (teach), help with people issues (relationship-builder) or assist with problem solving strategies (consultant). All these roles are important for a mentor.

2. a. Ability to project enthusiasm
   b. Understanding of motivation
   c. Ability to give constructive feedback

3. a. Define the problem
   b. Brainstorm ideas
   c. Prioritize ideas
   d. Develop an action plan
   e. Implement the plan
   f. Evaluate the plan
4. a. Problem centered

Notes

Chapter Four (page 111)

Answers will vary.

Chapter Five (page 124)

1. Choose from the following:
   ◆ Make being a mentor a privilege.
   ◆ Publicize mentoring success stories.
   ◆ Publicly recognize people who have participated in the program.
   ◆ Use current mentors to recruit potential mentors.
   ◆ Recruit the CEO as a mentor.

2. b. The mentor should simply try to ignore the discomfort and hope it will go away.

3. False—If a mentee has new skill areas that should be developed and the mentor does not have those skills, it is appropriate to find the mentee a mentor with the necessary skills. The original mentoring relationship could be retained if there are advantages to both partners to continue.

4. One of the main purposes of developing a mentoring relationship is to help the mentee improve knowledge and skills. This is best accomplished by the mentor demonstrating and modeling appropriate actions and by encouraging and supporting mentee growth rather than insisting that "my way is the way to do it."

   b. Experiential
   c. Self-directed
   d. Internally motivated
   e. Experience based

5. True—Most mentors have to work hard at allowing mentees to express their feelings and thoughts, so that they are not too directive.

Chapter Three (page 82)

1. a. Selective programs
     b. Volunteer programs
     c. All-organization programs

2. False—Top level commitment is vital for the initial start up of the program and for its continued success.

3. a. Determine the purpose.
     b. Seek organizational commitment.
     c. Identify the mentoring process to be used.
     d. Develop a program plan.
     e. Review the plan with decision-makers.
     f. Implement and evaluate the program.

4. Choose from the following:
   ◆ Written surveys
   ◆ Focus groups
   ◆ Measurement against set objectives
   ◆ Pre- and posttests
   ◆ Interviews
   ◆ Organizational records
   ◆ Competency lists
   ◆ Skills Demonstrations
   ◆ 360º feedback
   ◆ Log entries

5.   Don't forget to <u>celebrate</u> your successes!